Contemporary Candlewick Embroidery

Denise Giles

©2004 by Denise Giles

Published by

kp krause publications
An F+W Publications Company

700 East State Street • Iola, WI 54990-0001
715-445-2214 • 888-457-2873
www.krause.com

Our toll-free number to place an order or obtain
a free catalog is (800) 258-0929.

Library of Congress Catalog Number: 2004101563

ISBN: 0-87349-739-2

Designed by Donna Mummery

Edited by Nicole Gould

Printed in the United States of America

Acknowledgments

I would like to acknowledge appreciation to my beloved husband, Gary, for all his support, encouragement, and help; and to my son Daniel for his loving support and enthusiasm.

My editor, Nicole Gould, thank you for your hospitality, patience, and hard work creating this beautiful book.

Much appreciation also goes to photographer Kris Kandler for her expertise in creating the beautiful images. Thanks go to the expert staff at Krause Publications for their hard work in creating a quality product.

Special thanks goes to Julie Stephani for her mentoring spirit to me and so many other designers. I greatly appreciate the opportunity to create this book. I extend my appreciation to my Society of Craft Designer friends for their network support and encouragement.

Most importantly, thanks to the loving God who has given me the talent, opportunities, and strength to run the race.

Contents

Introduction

Researching the history of candlewick embroidery, I discovered that our ancestors used candlewick cotton—the same thread that they used to make wicks for candles—to create hand-stitched pieces for their homes. Colonial knots were created on an unbleached muslin background. Some stitchers went one step further, cutting the thread in between the stitches to make what they called "tufts." Traveling across the country in a covered wagon, space and supplies were limited, so early crafters were forced to use whatever materials were available.

After learning about candlewick embroidery a few years ago and seeing it done with only white thread, I wondered why no one had tried it with color. I saw many kits that combined colored crewel embroidery with white candlewick. Researching further, I discovered people using embroidery floss or pearl cotton to add color to their candlewick patterns. I decided to embrace this idea and expand upon it.

Modern life now affords so many choices for threads and materials. I loved the look of candlewick and wanted to take this old-fashioned needlework and revive it in the new millennium, with a fresh look.

I especially enjoy the texture of candlewick embroidery. It is such an easy craft, with only one main stitch to master—the French knot. I have added a few other stitches to give greater dimension to this contemporary embroidery. At the same time, I wanted to take it a little further than just adding color. I wanted to combine it with my favorite needlework—ribbon embroidery. In many of the projects in this book, you will find that I have added simple ribbon embroidery embellishments.

I also climbed "out of the box" and tried candlewick on many different fabrics, not just the traditional muslin. Candlewick embroidery really stands out when stitched on linen and even-weave fabrics. I also experimented with other fabrics, including colored cottons, denims, and flannels.

To help you get started, this book begins with step-by-step techniques and a stitch guide section. Next, you launch right into seven project chapters that represent seven rooms of a home. A variety of projects and patterns offer you a wide range of ideas to help spark your own creativity.

Greet your guests at the door with a stitched "welcome" sign in the Entryway. Fruity projects adorned with strawberries and green pears fill the Kitchen. Butterflies and dragonflies surround you in the Sun Room, while an eagle embellishes an oversized pillow in the Patriotic Den. Hearts and flowers fill a Romantic Bedroom and lovely vintage style pillows decorate the Guest Bedroom. Little baby ducks adorn the edge of a cute baby blanket in the Nursery.

Some projects will work up quickly while others will take a little more time to complete. However, when you finish, you will have an heirloom treasure that your loved ones will cherish for many years. I hope you enjoy this contemporary candlewick collection and create many of these lovely projects for your home.

Tools and Materials

Threads and Ribbons

Pearl cotton, size 8, and embroidery floss were used to stitch the candlewick embroidery projects throughout this book. For an elegant touch, ribbon embroidery was added to many of the projects. The threads and ribbons come in a variety of colors and can be found in your local craft or fabric stores.

Pearl cotton balls, are used in many of the projects in this book. Size 8 is the perfect size to make nice French knots for contemporary candlewick embroidery and is available in many colors. Cut the cotton into 24" lengths to work.

Six-strand embroidery floss can be used for this candlewick. The floss is actually separated and only four strands are used. Six-strand embroidery floss is readily available in many stores and can be substituted when you can't find the pearl cotton balls, size 8, in the needed colors.

Silk ribbon is used as accents in many of the projects. It comes in 4mm, 7mm, and 13mm sizes, in a wide variety of colors. Cut the ribbon into segments no longer than 12" to 18".

Before beginning your stitching, it is recommended that you pre-wash the ribbons in mild soap, hang them to dry, and press them on a silk setting.

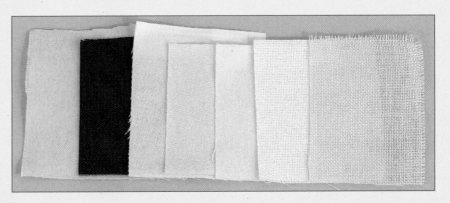

This ribbon bled onto the fabric because it was not pre-washed before stitching.

Fabric Choices

A variety of fabrics were used to stitch the projects shown throughout *Contemporary Candlewick*

Embroidery: linen, even-weave, colored cottons, flannel, and denim. Each will give a different look. When stitching on linen and even-weave fabrics, make sure to catch a thread of the fabric and do not go through the same hole when making your French knots.

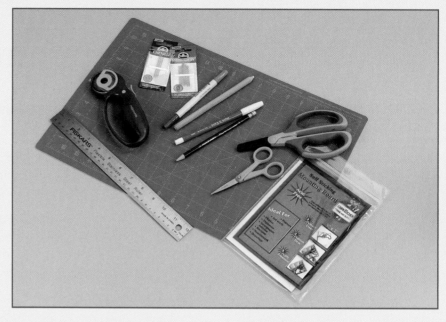

Hoops

For stitching your embroidery, a good embroidery hoop or frame is a must. A frame will help to keep your material taut and even, thus keeping your stitching neater and more accurate than holding it by hand. Many hoops and frames are equipped with stands and clamps to hold the embroidery piece, leaving your hands free. Your local craft or fabric store will carry many different hoops.

Round hoops consist of two parts, one smaller hoop that fits inside a larger hoop. The fabric is placed over the smaller hoop, and the larger hoop is placed over the fabric. A spring or screw on the outside hoop can be adjusted to fit snugly around the fabric. Round hoops come in many sizes and in various materials like metal, wood, or plastic.

Rectangle frames consist of four parts: two roller pieces at the top and bottom and two screw-type ends or flat ends with hole adjustments. Some roller bars have a strip of canvas for attaching the fabric and some have slits in the roller bars through which the fabric is passed. Each frame will come with instructions on how to attach fabrics.

Square frames come in a variety of sizes and are made from plastic tubing. They have four sections that snap together with four plastic clips.

Needles

Needles come in various sizes and styles. The higher the number of the needle, the smaller and finer the needle is.

Chenille needles are long-eyed needles with sharp points. Chenille needles are used for working heavy threads, fabrics, and silk ribbon embroidery. I recommend using sizes 20 and 22 for candlewick embroidery.

Embroidery needles are sharp needles with long, oval eyes. They are used for fine and medium surfaces. I recommended using sizes 1 and 2.

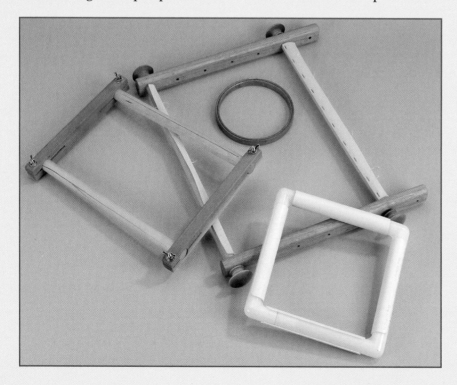

Beading needles are very fine needles with a tiny eye. They are strictly for beading and come in long and short sizes. Short needles are best for picking up one bead at a time. I recommend using a short size 10, which is easier to work with than the longer beading needles.

Marking Tools

Marking is a very important part of the process, so make sure you have the necessary tools for tracing and marking.

Marking pens are used for tracing your pattern to the fabric. Use a good fabric-marking pen with water-soluble ink, which can be removed with a damp cloth.

Chalk pencils are for marking a pattern on a dark fabric, such as marking the stars in the corner of the eagle pillow.

Tracing paper is necessary for tracing the patterns from the book so you can transfer the pattern to your fabric.

Pencils are used to trace the patterns to the tracing paper.

A light table is recommended for transferring the patterns to the fabric.

Mounting boards are used to back your needlework for framing. Foam core board can be used as a mounting board, or a pre-cut mounting board with a self-stick side can be purchased at your local craft store. They are available in many sizes.

Cutting Tools

A good cutting mat, acrylic ruler, and rotary cutter are recommended for cutting the fabric pieces for pillows and quilts. The mat and acrylic ruler have ¼" to 1" markings, which will help you keep the fabric pieces square and straight. You will also need a small, sharp, pointed pair of embroidery scissors and a good pair of fabric scissors.

Techniques

Tracing

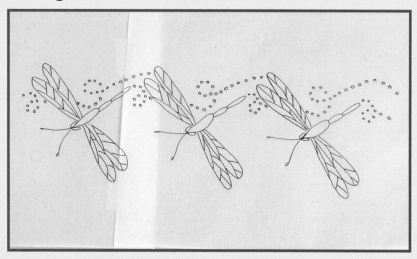

Use tracing paper and a #2 pencil to trace the pattern from the book. When the pattern is split on two pages, tape two sheets of tracing paper together and trace the pattern, matching the dotted line. Match up the dotted lines to complete the length of the pattern.

Transferring

After tracing your pattern to tracing paper, transfer to your fabric piece. Here are a few suggestions for the transfer:

A light table is one option. Tape the pattern to the light table, place the fabric over the pattern, and secure it with tape. Turn the light on. Trace the pattern using a fabric pen. Remove the tape and turn the light off. Begin your stitching.

A window can be used instead of a light table. Tape the pattern to the window and tape the fabric over the pattern. Trace the pattern with the fabric pen.

Dressmaker's carbon comes in light and dark colors. Tape your fabric to a smooth clean surface. Place the carbon, ink-side down, on top of the fabric, and then place the pattern on top and tape it in place. With a pencil, trace the pattern; mark all the lines, using enough pressure to transfer the design clearly.

Washing

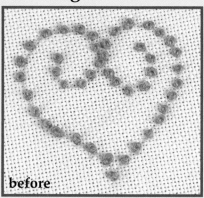

before

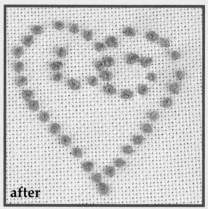

after

To clean your stitched piece, hand wash it in cold water with mild dish soap. Swish the piece around gently several times, but do not agitate it vigorously. A soft bristle

toothbrush can be used to scrub dirty spots as needed. Rinse well by soaking the piece in fresh changes of water several times. After thoroughly rinsing, lift the needlework from the water. Do not wring. Lay the needlework on a clean towel and roll it up like a jellyroll. Set it aside for a few minutes to let the towel absorb most of the water. Unroll the piece and place it face down on another clean dry towel. Iron the piece dry from the backside. Turn the needlework over and touch up the front. Leave the piece on the ironing board to finish drying overnight. If your silk ribbon becomes a little flat while ironing, spray it with a little water and use your fingers to reshape the ribbon. Allow the project to air dry.

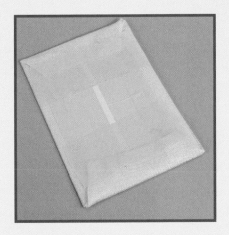

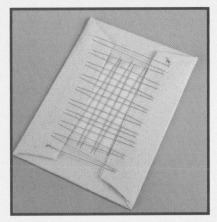

make sure it is still centered. Continue taping the sides, top, and bottom, and then the corners.

Lacing is another way of mounting your needlework to the board. Center the board on the back of the needlework.

Pull the fabric to the back. Starting at one end, work toward the other end, lacing from top to bottom using a needle and pearl cotton. Check to make sure the needlework is centered. Fold the corners of the fabric in and lace from side to side.

Mounting and Framing

You may choose to have your needlework professionally framed. With some of the larger pieces, I chose to have them framed. I was able to frame some of the smaller ones myself. Here are a few tips on mounting and framing.

Mounting

Use a self-stick mounting board or foam core board to mount your embroidery work. Lay your needlework piece face down, centering the mounting board over the needlework. Cut the fabric 1" to 2" larger than the mounting board. Pull the fabric to the back of the board in the center and tack it with a piece of tape. Pick the piece up and check the front to

Framing

To frame your own work after mounting the needlework, you will need the following:

❀ Frame
❀ Mat
❀ Second mounting board or foam core board to fit frame
❀ Brown paper
❀ Picture hanging kit that consists of screw eyes, wire, and picture hangers with nails
❀ Tape
❀ Glue
❀ Tools: scissors, wire cutters, and hammer

Take your needlework to a craft store to locate a matching mat and frame. After mounting your needlework to the mounting board (see above), center it in the mat frame, and tape it to the back of the mat. Place the piece in the frame and back it with a second piece of mounting board that fits the frame. Tape the board to the frame and cover the back with brown paper. Glue the paper to the frame around the edges.

Follow the directions that come with your picture hanging kit to hang the project.

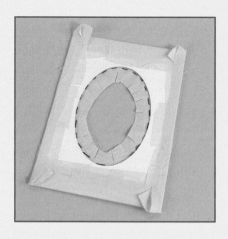

Mat Board Frames

To create your own fabric-covered mats for framing your needlework, follow these simple steps:

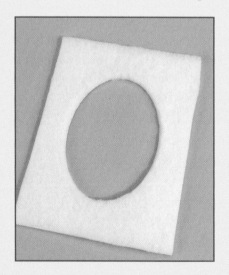

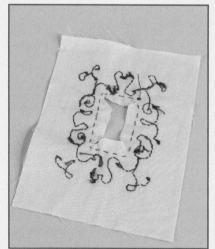

3 When using an oval opening, clip the fabric around the curve of the oval on the inside of the frame. Pull the fabric to the back on the sides, top, and bottom, and tape it in place.

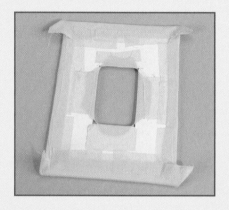

4 Remove the basting stitch from the center and pull the fabric to the back; tape it in place.

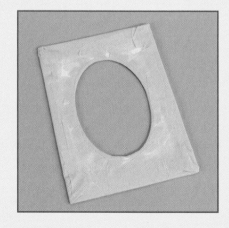

1 Apply spray adhesive to the mat board. Cover it with batting and trim the excess batting from edges and opening.

2 Baste a running stitch along the inside mat line of the stitched piece. This will help guide in the placement on the mat. Trim the excess fabric to ¾" on the outside of the mat. Trim the inside to ¾", clipping corners.

5 Pull the corners to the back and tape them in place.

Pillows

The following procedure is used for creating the pillows in this book:

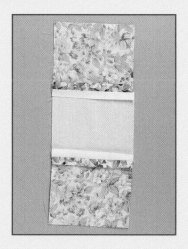

1 Pin and sew the short strips to the top and bottom of the center square. Press the seams open.

2 Pin and sew the long strips on the sides of the center piece. Press the seams open.

3 Pin the pillow back to the pillow front with right sides together. Sew a ⅝" seam allowance leaving an 8" opening on one side for turning.

4 Trim the excess fabric from the corners.

5 Turn the pillow covering right-side out and insert the pillow form. Close the pillow opening with whipstitches.

Step 2

Step 3

Step 4

Quilting

The quilts is this book are created with a few simple steps:

1 Spread the quilt batting out on a clean floor. Spread the finished quilt top over the batting. Randomly pin the top to the batting.

2 Baste the top to the batting around the edges with a long running stitch. Trim away any excess batting.

3 Spread the backing over the quilt top, right sides together. Pin around the edges and trim away the excess fabric from the edge of the quilt. Sew the layers together using a ⅝" seam allowance. Leave an opening on one edge. Trim the corners and turn right-side out. Close the opening using whipstitches. Spread the finished quilt out on the floor

again. Smooth and pin the layers together, starting in the center and working out toward the edges.

4 Tie the quilt using pearl cotton. Starting at the center of your quilt, take long stitches going through all three layers. Keep the distance between the ties about 4" apart. Cut in the center of the threads, between where the knots will be.

5 Tie each of the tails with square knots (see page 16). Trim the tails to the desired length. Leave at least ¾" tails to prevent unraveling of knots.

Stitch Guide

Stitches for Threads

If you are new to embroidery, I recommended that you do a practice sample to familiarize yourself with the stitches.

French Knot

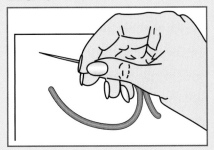

1 Bring your needle through the fabric to the front. Take the needle in your right hand, holding it firmly between your thumb and fingers.

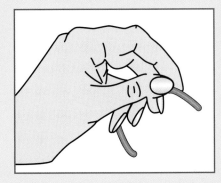

2 Grasp the thread in your left hand, about 2" from the fabric where the thread emerges.

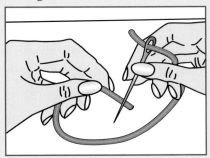

3 Place the needle against the topside of the thread, about ¼" from where it comes out of the fabric.

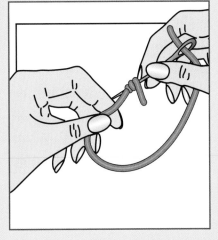

4 Wrap the thread away from you, three times around needle, keeping it tight with the left hand.

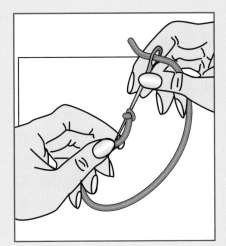

5 Keeping the thread taut, pull it toward you while lowering the point of the needle into the fabric, next to, but not in, the hole where it originally came out.

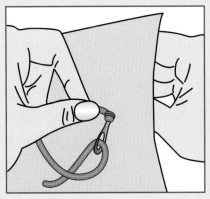

6 Push the needle into the fabric, keeping the thread firmly against the fabric while reaching around and grabbing the needle from the other side. Twist the needle counter-clockwise as you pull it through the fabric. This will keep the character of the knots intact. Pull all the way through the fabric, releasing the thread from your left hand as the knot is completed.

Ribbon Tip: Pre-Washing

Pre-wash and press all ribbons before stitching. This process doesn't take long and will help you to avoid disasters later!

1. Remove the ribbon from the card.
2. Hand wash the ribbons (especially the dark-colored ones) with mild dish soap in warm water.
3. Hang the ribbon to dry.
4. Press the ribbon with a low iron on a silk setting.

Colonial Knot

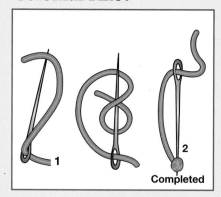

Bring the needle up at 1. Holding the thread in a backwards "C," insert the needle under the thread at top of the "C." Loop the thread over and under the needle, forming a figure 8. Hold the needle vertically and pull the knot firmly around the needle. Insert the needle at 2 as close as possible to 1, but not into the same hole. Hold the knot in place until the needle is pulled completely through the fabric.

A Colonial knot is an alternative to the French knot. It makes a slightly larger knot than the French knot and is a little more consistent.

Square Knot

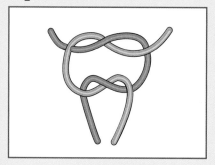

Take the right-hand thread over the left-hand thread and pull through. Next take the left-hand thread over the right-hand thread and pull it through to form the square knot.

Outline Stitch

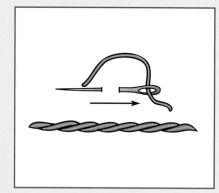

Bring the needle up through the fabric. With the thread to the left of the needle, insert the needle a short distance away on the line and bring the needle out again on the line. This stitch makes a fine line and is used around edges and for veining and detail lines.

Stem Stitch

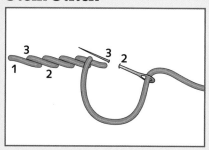

This stitch differs from the outline stitch in that the thread is held on the opposite side of the line. The needle is inserted to the right of the line and brought up to the left of the line, making a thick outline.

Buttonhole Stitch

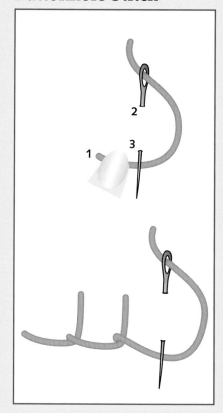

Working from left to right, bring the needle up through the fabric. Hold the thread under your left thumb and form a loop. Pass the needle through the fabric and over the looped thread. Repeat.

Satin Stitch

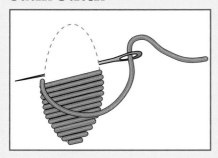

To form the stain stitch, straight stitches are worked side-by-side to fill small areas.

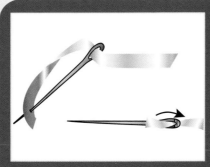
Lazy Daisy Stitch

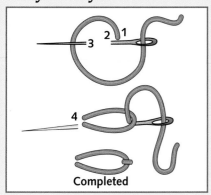

Come up through the fabric at 1 and form a loop. Go down at 2, close to 1. Bring the end of the needle up at 3 with the thread behind the needle. Go down at 4 to anchor the stitch.

Backstitch

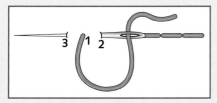

Place short stitches end-to-end for a slim outline. Come up at 1, take a small backward stitch, go down at 2, and come up at 3, always moving the needle forward under the fabric and coming up one stitch length ahead, ready to take another stitch back. Keep the stitches even.

Stitches for Ribbons

Ribbon Spider Web Rose

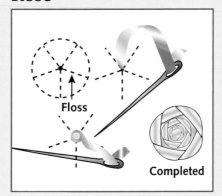

Draw a circle on the fabric the desired size of the finished rose. For the web, use floss or pearl cotton. Come up in the center and stitch five evenly-spaced spokes with straight stitches, connecting in the center to form a web. Bring the ribbon up through the fabric near the center of the web. Weave the ribbon over and under the spokes until the spokes are completely covered. Weave the ribbon tightly at first, then loosen it toward the outer edge, letting the ribbon twist to form petals. Take the needle back through the fabric on the edge of the rose and anchor it to the back of the fabric.

Ribbon Lazy Daisy Stitch

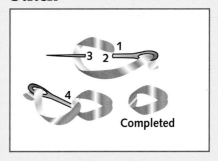

The ribbon lazy daisy stitch is made in the same way as the thread lazy daisy stitch, the only difference is in the way the ribbon lays to make leaves and petals. Bring the needle up at 1 and down at 2 close to 1. Next bring needle up at 3 to catch the ribbon loop. Make sure the ribbon is not twisted and anchor the loop at 4.

Japanese Ribbon Stitch

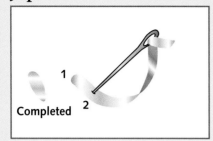

Come up at 1, lay the ribbon flat on the fabric and pierce the center of the ribbon at 2. Gently pull the needle through the ribbon to the back. The edges of the ribbon will curl and form a point. Be careful not to pull too tight or you will lose the effect of this stitch. Vary the leaves and petals by adjusting the length and tension of the ribbon before piercing.

Leaf Ribbon Stitch

Mark the shape of your leaf on the fabric. Starting at the top come up at 1, go down at 2, making a short straight stitch. Come up at 3, go down at 4. Come back up at 5, bring the needle over the ribbon, anchoring at 6. Follow the outline of the leaf and repeat steps 3-6.

Straight Stitch

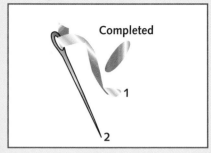

Come up at 1, go down at 2, making the stitch the desired length.

Ribbon Tip: Knotting the Ribbon End

1. Fold the loose end of the ribbon over ¼".
2. Push the needle through both thicknesses of the folded ribbon.
3. Pull the needle completely through the ribbon, forming a knot at the end of the ribbon length.

Ribbon leaf stitch, French knots, satin stitch.

French knots, stem stitch, thread lazy daisy stitch.

Ribbon spider web rose, Japanese ribbon stitch, ribbon lazy daisy stitch, stem stitch, French knots.

Outline stitch, satin stitch, Colonial knots, French knots.

French knots, stem stitch, ribbon lazy daisy stitch, spider web rose.

Entryway

1

The entryway creates your guests' first impression of your home. Welcome them with this lovely stitched welcome sign. Your smiling faces reflected in the hydrangea mirror will make them feel at home. A clock shows how time flies when you're having fun with family and friends; a trinket box holds a little treat for the sweet tooth.

Welcome Sign

Vine Clock

Hydrangea Mirror

English Ivy Keepsake Box

Design Dimensions: 11" x 5"

Welcome Sign

Give your guests a warm welcome with this French-knotted welcome sign detailed with a lovely grapevine border pattern. The word "welcome" is filled with French knots, and a simple repeated grapevine border pattern is added to complete the sign. Show off your finished piece in a nice frame and add a grapevine for just the right touch to your entryway.

Materials

18" x 15" piece of ivory 32-ct. linen fabric*

6-strand embroidery floss*: Deer Brown #841, Beige Rope #842, Silver Green #3052, Tweed Green #3053, and Dark Antique Violet #3740

Embroidery needle

Frame, mat board, tape, and foam core board

Miscellaneous items: embroidery hoop, scissors, tracing paper, pencil, light table, and disappearing ink pen

Products used: linen by Charles Craft®; embroidery floss by DMC® Corp.

Instructions

Trace the pattern on pages 100 and 101, matching the dotted line to complete the full pattern.

Transfer the pattern to the center of the linen fabric. (See page 10.)

Stitch the welcome sign pattern. Use four strands of floss for all stitches. Refer to the stitch guide on pages 15 to 19.

Welcome

1. Outline stitch the letters using Deer Brown floss #841.
2. Fill the letters with French knots using Beige Rope floss #842.
3. Backstitch the rectangle border around the "welcome" using Deer Brown floss #841.

Grapevine Border

1. Stem stitch the vine using Silver Green floss #3052.
2. Lazy daisy stitch the leaves using Tweed Green floss #3053.
3. Stitch the grape clusters with French knots using Dark Antique Violet floss #3740.

Finishing Touches

1. Clean your stitched embroidery piece. See washing tips on page 10.
2. Frame the finished pieces as desired. See tips on framing, page 11.

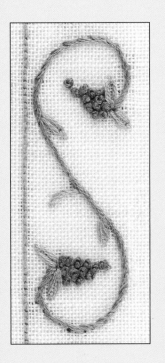

Design Dimensions: 4⅛" circle

Vine Clock

For a lovely accent in your entryway, take time to be creative with this simple stitched clock pattern framed in a wooden bezel clock. Family and friends will definitely be checking this clock—but not because they want to leave!

Instructions

Trace the pattern on page 99 onto paper.
Transfer the pattern to the center of the linen fabric. (See page 10.)
Stitch the clock face pattern. Use four strands of embroidery floss for all stitches. Refer to the stitch guide on pages 15 to 19.

Materials

Bezel clock with a 4" diameter stitching area*
8" square piece of 28-ct. ivory linen*
6-strand embroidery floss*: Medium Lilac #3041 and Insect Green #3347
Embroidery needle
Miscellaneous items: tracing paper, pencil, light table, disappearing ink pen, embroidery hoop, and scissors

*Products used: bezel clock by Sudberry House; linen by Wichelt Imports; floss by DMC® Corp.

Clock Face

1. Outline stitch the vine using Insect Green floss #3347.
2. Outline stitch the outline of the leaves in positions 12, 3, 6, and 9 using Medium Lilac floss #3041.
3. Fill these sections and the hourly points with French knots using Medium Lilac floss #3041.

Finishing Touches

Assembling the clock:

1. Carefully remove the bezel from the front of the clock by pulling it straight out. Remove the center. Remove the nut in the center, then the mounting board.
2. Center the design over the board and stitch a running stitch ¼" larger than the board. Pull the thread to tighten it around the mounting board and secure stitch it to the back. Trim the excess fabric and cut a ¼" hole in the center.
3. Reassemble the clock by pushing the mounting board all the way down the shaft, and then add the washer and the nut. Add the clock hands.
4. Check the manufacturer's instructions for assembling the hands. Place four pieces of double-sided tape on the wood rim inside the clock; this will help hold the mount board in place. Replace the assembled clock into the frame. Carefully replace the bezel on the front of the clock.

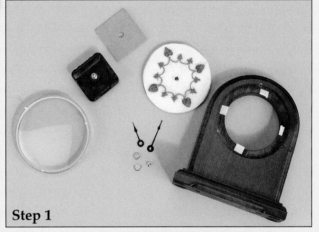

Step 1

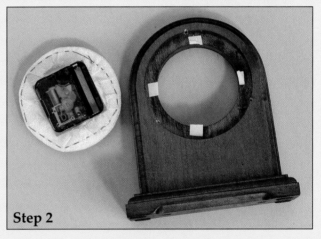

Step 2

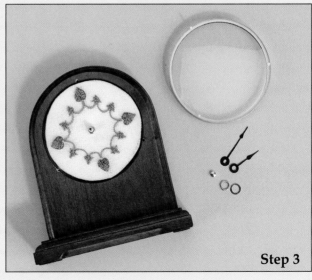

Step 3

Materials

Wall mirror with 5" x 7" design area*
8" x 10" piece of 28-ct. ivory linen*
6-strand embroidery floss*: Lilac #3042,
    Medium Lilac #3041, Dark Moss Green
    #469
4mm silk ribbon*: 1 yd. Olive #508; 3 yd.
    each Jungle Green #653 and Dusty
    Purple #571
Embroidery needle
Miscellaneous items: tracing paper,
    pencil, light table, disappearing ink pen,
    embroidery hoop, and scissors

*Products used: mirror #20091 by Sudberry
House; linen by Wichelt Imports; floss by DMC®
Corp.; silk ribbon by Bucilla® Plaid Enterprises

Hydrangea Mirror

For a nice reflection in the entryway, this mirror has a ribbon-embroidered hydrangea surrounded by a French-knotted border entwined with a leafy vine. It's handy for those last minute makeup and hair checks as you leave the house.

Design Dimensions: 5" x 7"

Instructions

Trace the pattern on page 98 onto paper.

Transfer the pattern to the center of the linen fabric. (See page 10.)

Stitch the border and hydrangea patterns. Use four strands of embroidery floss on all stitches. Refer to the stitch guide on pages 15 to 19.

Border

1. Outline stitch the border using Lilac floss #3042.
2. Fill the border with French knots using Medium Lilac floss #3041.
3. Stem stitch the vine using Dark Moss floss #469.
4. Lazy daisy stitch the leaves on the vine using Jungle Green silk ribbon #653.

Hydrangea Flower

1. Satin stitch the stem using Dark Moss floss #469.
2. Leaf ribbon stitch the leaves using Jungle Green silk ribbon #653.
3. Straight stitch the flower petals using Dusty Purple silk ribbon #571.
4. Stitch the flower centers with French knots using Jungle Green silk ribbon #653.
5. Fill the top of the flower with French knots using Jungle Green #653 and Olive #508 silk ribbon.

Finishing Touches

1. Carefully remove the two mounting boards from the frame. Some frames may not come with two mounting boards. If this is the case, use the mounting board as a pattern to cut another piece of mounting board the same size.
2. Center the clean needlework over one mounting board. Trim the excess fabric to about ½" from the edge of the mounting board. See tips for washing on page 10.
3. Turn the fabric to the back and secure it with tape or lace with floss from side to side for a tight fit. Refer to the lacing and taping samples on page 11.
4. Clean the glass, place the needlework next to the glass, and then place the second mounting board over the needlework.

Design Dimensions: 5" circle

English Ivy Keepsake Box

A keepsake box in the entryway is a great place to keep your keys so you always know where they are. I tend to lose my keys if I don't put them in the same place every time. This Broider box has a 5" opening to display the simple French-knotted ivy design with two shades of green. This pattern might also be used in a quilt block or on a pillow.

Materials

Broider box with 5" round design area*
8" square piece of 28-ct. ivory linen*
Pearl cotton balls*, size 8: Hunter Green #3346, Insect Green #3347, Hare Brown #840
5½" square piece of batting
Spray adhesive
Mounting board
Embroidery needle
Miscellaneous items: tracing paper, pencil, light table, disappearing ink pen, tape, embroidery hoop, and scissors

*Products used: Broider Box #99051 by Sudberry House; linen by Wichelt Imports; pearl cotton by DMC® Corp.

Instructions

Trace the pattern on page 99 onto paper.
Transfer the pattern to the center of the linen fabric. (See page 10.)
Stitch the leaves and vine using one strand of pearl cotton. Four strands of embroidery floss may be substituted in place of the pearl cotton. Refer to the stitch guide on pages 15 to 19.

Vine

Outline stitch the vine using Hare Brown pearl cotton #840.

Leaves

1. Outline stitch every other leaf and fill with French knots using Hunter Green pearl cotton #3346.
2. Outline stitch the remainder of the leaves and fill with French knots using Insect Green pearl cotton #3347.

Finishing Touches

1. Wash the stitched piece to remove any dirt and fabric pen markings. See tips for washing on page 10.
2. Open the box and bend back the framer points to remove the mount board. Trace the board on a second piece of mount board and cut it out to be used as the backing. This will make a nice finish for the inside of your box.
3. Apply spray adhesive to one of the mount boards and place the batting on top of the sprayed mount board.
4. Center the clean and pressed stitching over the batting. Turn the fabric edges to the back and tape them in place. See tips on page 11.
5. With the box open, place the needlework inside and then add the second mount board. Push the prong back against the board.

2

Fruit-full Kitchen

The smell of pie cooking in the oven and a freshly iced cake under glass are just a few of the fond memories I have of my grandmother's kitchen. She always kept a bowl of fresh fruit on the counter. When the fruit became too ripe, it was turned into a delicious pie and enjoyed with a scoop of vanilla ice cream.

In this chapter are some fruity accents for the kitchen with strawberries and pears. For holding those old family favorite recipes, create a recipe box with a stitched strawberry vine. Also, stitch a strawberry cluster on the front of a dishtowel or mount the cluster in a frame.

For a nice table setting, a pear border is stitched along the edge of the place mats and a pear is stitched on one corner of each napkin.

Strawberry Recipe Box

Strawberry Dishtowel and Frame

Pear Place Mat & Napkin Set

Design Dimensions: 4" x 5"

Strawberry Recipe Box

Store your favorite recipes in this oak box with the word "Recipes" stitched in French knots, surrounded by a strawberry vine border. For an elegant touch, the leaves and flowers are stitched with silk ribbon. Seed beads are added to the center of each blossom. Beads are also used for the seeds on each strawberry.

Materials
8" x 10" piece of linen in Buttermilk*
Recipe box with 4" x 6" design area*
Pearl cotton balls*, size 8: China Red #304, Medium Terracotta #356, Insect Green #3347
Silk ribbon*: 4 yd. of 4mm Light Emerald #642 and 1½ yd. of 4mm White #003
Frosted Autumn glass beads #62044*
Embroidery needle and beading needle
Miscellaneous items: tracing paper, pencil, light table, disappearing ink pen, tape, card stock paper, embroidery hoop, and scissors

*Products used: recipe box #99088 by Sudberry House; linen by Wichelt Imports; floss by DMC® Corp.; silk ribbon by Bucilla® Plaid Enterprises; beads by Mill Hill

Instructions

Trace the pattern on page 100 onto paper. *Transfer* the pattern to the center of the linen fabric. (See page 10.)
Stitch the recipe box pattern using one strand of pearl cotton. Four strands of embroidery floss may be substituted in place of the pearl cotton. Refer to the stitch guide on pages 15 to 19.

Recipes

1. Outline stitch the letters using Medium Terracotta pearl cotton #356.
2. Fill the letters with French knots using Medium Terracotta pearl cotton #356.

Strawberry Border

1. Outline stitch the strawberries using China Red pearl cotton #304.
2. Fill the strawberries with French knots using China Red pearl cotton #304.
3. Outline stitch the vines using Insect Green pearl cotton #3347.
4. Stitch the leaves with the leaf ribbon stitch using 4mm Light Emerald silk ribbon #642.
5. Lazy daisy stitch the flowers and buds using White silk ribbon #003.

6. Japanese ribbon stitch the bud leaves using Light Emerald silk ribbon #642.
7. Sew three Autumn beads in each flower center using a beading needle and thread.
8. Attach additional Autumn beads for the strawberry seeds.

Finishing Touches

1. Clean the stitched embroidery piece. See page 10 for washing tips.
2. Bend out the framer point on the inside of the box lid. Remove the mounting board and clear acrylic sheet from the top of the recipe box. Peel the protective paper from the acrylic sheet.
3. Cut a piece of card stock paper the same size as the mounting board; this will be used to cover the back of the mounting board.
4. Center the stitched linen over the mounting board and trim the excess fabric back to 1" from the mounting board edges. Pull the fabric taut to the back; tape it in place on the back of the board. See mounting board tips on page 11.
5. Clean the clear acrylic sheet and place it inside the lid. Next, place the mounted stitched board and the cardstock paper inside the lid. Push the framer points back in place. Fill the box with your favorite recipes.

Design Dimensions Frame: 3" x 4"
Design Dimensions Towel: 4½" x 6"

Strawberry Dishtowel & Frame

Enjoy your morning coffee with strawberries and cream. Add accents of strawberries to your kitchen decor with this delightful cluster of strawberries stitched on a dishtowel with a textured corner border; or, frame the same strawberry cluster stitched on Buttermilk linen fabric.

Materials

1 ecru-colored dishtowel with a 4½"x 6" 14-ct. stitching area*
OR an 8" x 10" piece of linen in Buttermilk*
Pearl cotton balls*, size 8: China Red #304, Medium Terracotta #356, Insect Green #3347
Silk ribbon*: 4 yd. 4mm Light Emerald #642 and 1½ yd. 4mm White #003
Frosted Autumn glass beads #62044*
Embroidery needle and beading needle
Miscellaneous items: tracing paper, pencil, light table, disappearing ink pen, tape, card stock paper, embroidery hoop, and scissors

*Products used: Showcase huck towel by Charles Craft®; linen by Wichelt Imports; pearl cotton by DMC® Corp.; silk ribbon by Bucilla® Plaid Enterprises; beads by Mill Hill

Instructions

Trace the pattern on page 101 onto paper. If you are making the framed piece, only trace the center of the design.

Transfer the pattern to the center of the 14-ct. stitching area on the towel or the linen. (See page 10.)

Stitch the pattern using one strand of pearl cotton. Four strands of embroidery floss may be substituted using the same color numbers as the pearl cotton. Refer to the stitch guide on pages 15 to 19.

Corner *(Shown on dishtowel)*

Stitch each block with nine French knots using Medium Terracotta pearl cotton #356.

Strawberry Cluster

1. Outline stitch the strawberries using China Red pearl cotton #304.
2. Fill the strawberries with French knots using China Red pearl cotton #304.
3. Outline stitch the vines using Insect Green pearl cotton #3347.
4. Stitch the leaves with ribbon leaf stitch using 4mm Light Emerald silk ribbon #642.
5. Lazy daisy stitch the flowers and buds with White silk ribbon #003.
6. Japanese ribbon stitch the bud leaves using Light Emerald silk ribbon #642.
7. Sew three Autumn beads in each flower center using beading needle and thread.
8. Attach additional Autumn beads for the strawberry seeds.

Finishing Touches

1. Clean the stitched embroidery pieces to remove any dirt and fabric pen markings. See page 10 for washing tips.
2. If you are framing the design, cut a piece of mount board to fit your frame. Center the stitching over the mount board. Pull the excess fabric to the back and tape it in place. For framing tips, see page 11.

Design Dimensions Place Mat: 3" x 9"
Design Dimensions Napkin: 3" x 3"

Pear Place Mat & Napkin Set

With fruit being a popular decorating element for the kitchen, try setting your table with pears. Create this placemat and napkin set embellished with a simple border and French-knotted pears with silk ribbon leaves.

Materials

(for two place mat and napkin sets)

2 yd. cotton fabric in wheat color

Pearl cotton balls*, size 8: Vanilla #746, Insect Green #3347, Lettuce Head Green #3348, and Hare Brown #840

Silk ribbon*: 4mm Olive #509

Embroidery needle

Sewing machine

Wheat color sewing thread

Miscellaneous items: tracing paper, pencil, light table, disappearing ink pen, tape, embroidery hoop, and scissors

Tools: scissors, cutting mat, acrylic ruler, and rotary cutter*

Products used: pearl cotton balls by DMC® Corp.; silk ribbon by Bucilla® Plaid Enterprises; tools by Fiskars®

Instructions for Place Mat

Cut the fabric into four 13¼" x 19¼" pieces for the place mats

Trace the place mat pattern on page 102 onto paper.

Mark the seamline with a fabric pen ⅝" from the edges of one of the place mat fabric pieces.

Transfer the border pattern 1" from the seamline to the left side of the place mat.

Stitch the pear border pattern using one strand of pearl cotton. Four strands of embroidery floss may be substituted using the same color number as the pearl cotton. Refer to the stitch guide on pages 15 to 19.

Vine

1. Outline stitch the vine using Hare Brown pearl cotton #840.
2. Stitch the leaves with French knots using Lettuce Head Green pearl cotton #3348.

Pears

1. Outline stitch the pear using Insect Green pearl cotton #3347.
2. Fill the highlights on the pears with French knots using Vanilla pearl cotton #746.
3. Fill the rest of the pear with French knots using Lettuce Head Green pearl cotton #3348.
4. Satin stitch the pear stem using Hare Brown pearl cotton #840.
5. Stitch the pear leaves with the leaf ribbon stitch using 4mm Olive silk ribbon.

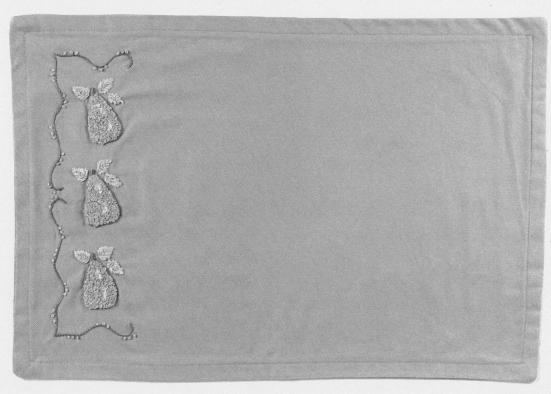

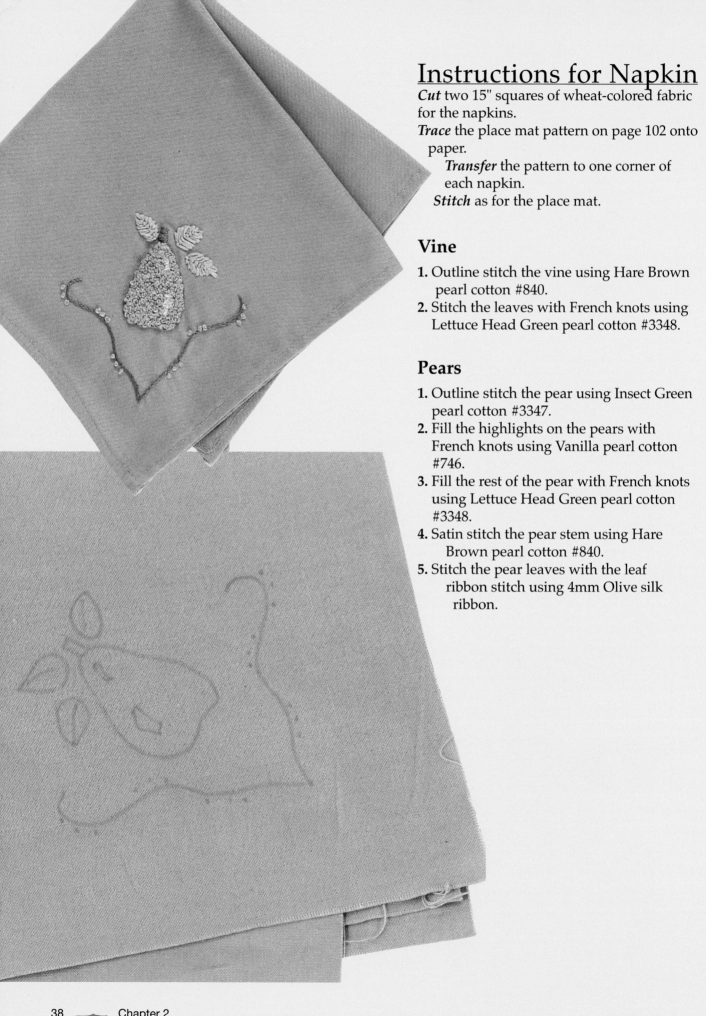

Instructions for Napkin

Cut two 15" squares of wheat-colored fabric for the napkins.

Trace the place mat pattern on page 102 onto paper.

   Transfer the pattern to one corner of each napkin.

   Stitch as for the place mat.

Vine

1. Outline stitch the vine using Hare Brown pearl cotton #840.
2. Stitch the leaves with French knots using Lettuce Head Green pearl cotton #3348.

Pears

1. Outline stitch the pear using Insect Green pearl cotton #3347.
2. Fill the highlights on the pears with French knots using Vanilla pearl cotton #746.
3. Fill the rest of the pear with French knots using Lettuce Head Green pearl cotton #3348.
4. Satin stitch the pear stem using Hare Brown pearl cotton #840.
5. Stitch the pear leaves with the leaf ribbon stitch using 4mm Olive silk ribbon.

Finishing Touches

For the place mat: With right sides together, place the place mat back over the front, and sew them together, using a ⅝" seam allowance. Leave a 5" opening on one end. Trim the corners and turn the place mat right-side out. Close the opening with whipstitches. Press and top stitch all edges ½" from the edge of the place mat.

For the napkin: Turn the edges of the napkin under ¼" twice and sew along the edge. Repeat for each napkin.

3 Sun Room

My grandmother's huge, screened-in porch across one end of the house was filled with treasures. Wicker furniture and plants gave the room a warm, welcome feel. As kids, our favorite part of the room was a large, old, black trunk full of toys. We played there for countless hours, letting our imaginations run wild.

Bring the outdoors in by filling your favorite sun room with beautiful accents of butterflies and dragonflies. Create accent pillows for your wicker chairs. Serve your guests some iced tea with a lovely tray and frame your favorite photo with a stitched mat frame.

Dragonfly Pillow

Butterfly Pillow

Butterfly & Dragonfly Breakfast Tray

Butterfly & Dragonfly Mat Frame

Design Dimensions: 13½" x 5"

Dragonfly Pillow

Capture the dragonfly leaving his trail behind with the texture of French knots stitched in a repeated pattern. Add a lavender fringe to the edge of the stitched panel. Sew the panel to pistachio green fabric to create a lovely pillow.

Materials

½ yd. pistachio green fabric*
¼ yd. white 32-ct. linen fabric
1 yd. quartz-colored fringe, 1" wide*
14" square pillow insert*
6-strand embroidery floss*: Cotton Cream #822, Pale Lilac #3743, Lilac #3042, Insect Green #3347, and Lettuce Head Green #3348
Green and purple sewing threads
Embroidery needle
Miscellaneous items: sewing machine, tracing paper, pencil, light table, disappearing ink pen, embroidery hoop, and scissors
Tools: cutting mat, acrylic ruler, and rotary cutter*

Products used: fabric by Waverly; linen by Charles Craft®; embroidery floss by DMC® Corp.; trim by Wrights®; Poly-fil Soft Touch® pillow insert by Fairfield; tools by Fiskars®

Instructions

Cut the fabric into two 15¼" squares. Cut the linen into one 8" x 15¼" piece.

Trace the pattern on pages 104 and 105 onto paper, matching the dotted lines to complete the full pattern. (See page 10.)

Transfer the pattern to the center of the linen strip. (See page 10.)

Stitch the pattern. Use four strands of embroidery floss on all the stitches except the lines inside the wings, which only require two strands of embroidery floss. Refer to the stitch guide on pages 15 to 19.

Dragonfly Body

1. Outline stitch the body using Insect Green floss #3347.
2. Satin stitch the eyes using Insect Green floss #3347.
3. Fill the dragonfly body with French knots, using Lettuce Head Green floss #3348.

Step 3

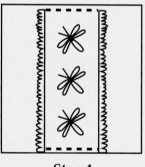

Step 4

Dragonfly Wings

1. Outline stitch the wing using Lilac floss #3042.
2. Outline stitch the inside lines of the wing using two strands of Pale Lilac floss #3743.

Trail

Stitch the trail with French knots using Cotton Cream floss #822.

Finishing Touches

1. Turn the sides of the cleaned, stitched, linen piece under ¼". See washing tips on page 10.
2. Cut two 15¼" pieces of fringe. To keep the trim from unraveling, tape the cut ends.
3. Pin the trim to the edges and hand tack it to the linen piece.
4. Center and pin the linen piece right-side up to the front of one fabric square. Baste at the top and bottom.
5. Pin the pillow back on the pillow front, with right sides together. Sew all sides with a ⅝" seam, leaving an 8" opening on one side for turning. Trim the excess fabric from the corners. Turn the pillow right-side out.
6. Insert the pillow form. Whipstitch the opening of the pillow closed. Refer to the pillow steps on page 13.

Design Dimensions: 4½" x 5½"

Materials

½ yd. pistachio green fabric*
14" x 18" piece of white 25-ct. even-weave
    needlework fabric
16" square pillow insert*
6-strand embroidery floss*: Mauve Violet #155,
    Light Blue Violet #156, Dark Blue Violet #158,
    Insect Green #3347, and Hunter Green #3346,
    two skeins of each color
4mm silk ribbon*: Jungle Green #653, Lilac #009,
    and Lavender #024
Green sewing thread
Embroidery needle
Miscellaneous items: sewing machine, tracing
    paper, pencil, light table, disappearing ink pen,
    embroidery hoop, and scissors
Tools: cutting mat, acrylic ruler, and rotary cutter*

*Products used: fabric by Waverly; needlework fabric by
DMC® Corp.; silk ribbon by Bucilla® Plaid Enterprises;
trim by Wrights®; Poly-fil Soft Touch® pillow insert by
Fairfield; tools by Fiskars®

Butterfly Pillow

I enjoy early springtime and the arrival of returning monarch butterflies … returning to beautiful flowers after their winter hiatus in South America. To create a lovely combination, add texture to your pillow with this striking French-knotted butterfly and an elegant ribbon-embroidered vine.

Instructions

Cut the green fabric into one 17¼" square piece. Cut two 8½" x 5⅝" strips with the fabric grain, and two strips 17¼" x 5⅝" across the fabric grain. Cut the needlework fabric into one 8½" square.

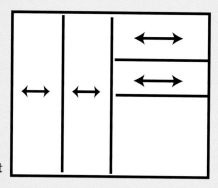

Trace the butterfly pattern on page 103 onto paper.

Transfer the butterfly pattern to the center of the needlework fabric. (See page 10.)

Stitch the butterfly pattern using four strands of embroidery floss for all stitches. Refer to the stitch guide on pages 15 to 19.

Butterfly Body

1. Outline stitch the body using Hunter Green floss #3346.
2. Satin stitch the eyes using Hunter Green floss #3346.
3. Fill the butterfly body with French knots, using Insect Green floss #3347.

Butterfly Wings

1. Outline stitch the wings using Dark Blue Violet floss #158.
2. Fill the inside section of the wings with French knots using Mauve Violet floss #155.
3. Fill the center section of the wings with French knots using Light Blue Violet floss #156.
4. Fill the small teardrop shapes on the outer sections of the wings with French knots using Light Blue Violet floss #156.
5. Finish filling the outer sections of the wings with French knots using Dark Blue Violet floss #158.

Pillow Top

1. Sew the green fabric strips to the clean needlework square using ⅝" seams. See tips for washing on page 10.
2. Pin and sew the short strips to the top and bottom of the butterfly square. Trim the seams to ¼" and press the seams toward the green fabric. Pin and sew the long strips on the sides of center piece. Trim the seams to ¼" and press the seams toward the outside edge. See page 13.

3. Topstitch along the edge of the green fabric next to the center square. This will give a nice finished look to your pillow.

Ribbon-Embroidered Vine

Trace the ribbon pattern. On each side of the needlework square, center the pattern and mark it on the green fabric.

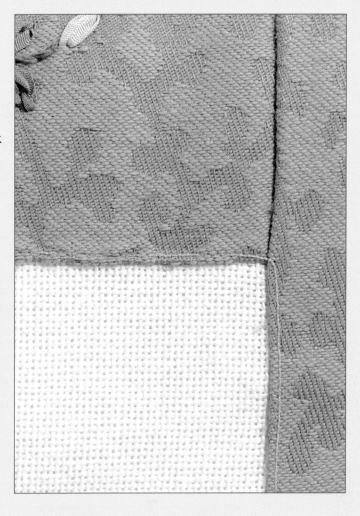

Embroider the ribbon pattern. Refer to the stitch guide on pages 15 to 19.

1. Stitch the flower center with French knots using Light Blue Violet Floss #156.
2. Stem stitch the vines using Hunter Green floss #3346.
3. Lazy daisy stitch the leaves using Jungle Green silk ribbon #653.
4. Lazy daisy stitch the flower buds using Lilac #009 and Lavender #024 silk ribbon
5. Straight stitch the flower petals using Lilac #009 and Lavender #024 silk ribbon.

See the embroidery pattern on page 103 and the photo for color placement.

Finishing Touches

1. Pin the pillow back to the pillow front, right sides together.
2. Sew a ⅝" seam allowance leaving an 8" opening on one side for turning. Trim the excess fabric from the corners. Turn right-side out.
3. Insert the pillow form. Close the pillow opening using whipstitches. See pillow steps on page 13.

Design Dimensions: 7" x 10"

Butterfly & Dragonfly Breakfast Tray

Butterflies and dragonflies under glass, adorning this wood tray, will help you serve your guests in style. Violet French knots fill the butterflies while turquoise French knots fill the dragonfly bodies. The dragonfly wings are outline stitched in shades of green.

Materials

Oak finish petite tray with oval design area*
14" x 18" piece of white even-weave
  needlework fabric*
6-strand embroidery floss*: Granny Smith
  Apple #907, Apple Green #906, Green
  Turquoise #3849, Wisteria Violet #340,
  Iris Violet #3746, Ecru
Embroidery needle
Miscellaneous items: scissors, paper,
  pencil, light table, disappearing ink pen,
  and embroidery hoop

Products used: petite oval tray #65008 by Sudberry House; even-weave needlework fabric #3865 and embroidery floss by DMC® Corp.

Instructions

Cut the fabric into a 14" x 10" piece.

Trace the pattern on page 106 onto paper.

Transfer the pattern to the center of the needlework fabric. (See page 10.)

Stitch the pattern. Use four strands of embroidery floss for all stitches except the lines inside the dragonfly wings. For the lines inside the dragonfly wings, use only two strands of embroidery floss. Refer to the stitch guide on pages 15 to 19.

Dragonflies

1. Outline stitch the body using Green Turquoise floss #3849.
2. Satin stitch the eyes using Green Turquoise floss #3849.
3. Fill the body with French knots, using Green Turquoise floss #3849.
4. Outline stitch the wings using Apple Green floss #906.
5. Outline stitch the inside wing lines using Granny Smith Apple floss #907.

Large Butterfly

1. Outline the body with outline stitch using Granny Smith Apple floss #907.
2. Satin stitch the eyes using Granny Smith Apple floss #907.
3. Fill the body with French knots using Granny Smith Apple floss #907.
4. Outline stitch the wings using Iris Violet floss #3746.
5. Fill the outer sections of the wings with French knots using Iris Violet floss #3746.
6. Fill the inner sections of the wings with French knots using Wisteria Violet floss #340.

Finishing Touches

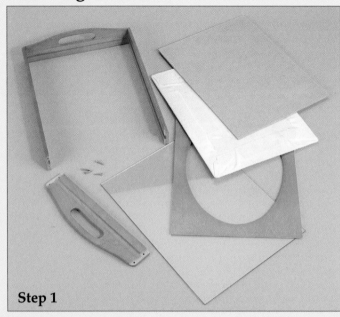

Step 1

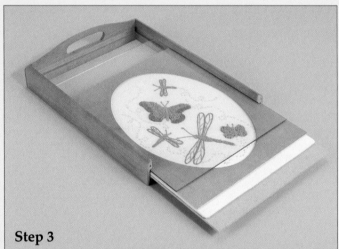

Step 3

Step 4

Small Butterfly

1. Outline stitch the body using Granny Smith Apple floss #907.
2. Satin stitch the eyes using Granny Smith Apple floss #907.
3. Fill the body with French knots using Granny Smith Apple floss #907.
4. Outline stitch the wings using Iris Violet floss #4746.
5. Fill the small sections on the wings with French knots using Iris Violet floss #3746.
6. Fill the wings with French knots using Wisteria Violet floss #340.

Trail

Stitch the trail with French knots using Ecru floss.

Finishing Touches

1. Remove the screws from one end of the tray with a small Phillips screwdriver and carefully slide out the glass, mat, mounting board, and back.
2. Center the clean finished needlework on the mat. See tips for washing on page 10. Wrap the needlework around the mounting board and secure it to the back with wide tape. See taping mat board page 11.
3. Clean the glass. Reassemble the tray, inserting the glass first, followed by the mat, the needlework on the mounting board, and the baseboard. Slide into the grooves.
4. Reassemble the end with the screws.

Design Dimensions: 4½" x 5½"

Materials

8" x 10" oak picture frame
8" x 10" mat board with a 5" x 7" opening
14" x 18" piece of white even-weave
   needlework fabric*
6-strand embroidery floss*: Granny Smith
   Apple #907, Apple Green #906, Green
   Turquoise #3849, Wisteria Violet #340, Iris
   Violet #3746, Ecru
Batting
Embroidery needle
Miscellaneous items: scissors, paper, pencil,
   light table, disappearing ink pen, spray
   adhesive, tape, and embroidery hoop

*Products used: even-weave needlework fabric
#3865 and embroidery floss by DMC® Corp.*

Butterfly & Dragonfly Mat Frame

Butterflies and dragonflies will flutter around your favorite photo with this stitched mat board. Notice how this stitched mat coordinates nicely with the breakfast tray.

Instructions

Cut the fabric into a 14" x 10" piece.

Trace the pattern on page 107 onto paper.

Transfer the pattern to the center of the needlework fabric. (See page 10.)

Stitch the pattern. Use four strands of embroidery floss on all stitches except the lines inside the wings. For those lines use two strands of embroidery floss. Refer to the stitch guide on pages 15 to 19.

Dragonflies

1. Outline stitch the body using Green Turquoise floss #3849.
2. Satin stitch the eyes using Green Turquoise floss #3849.
3. Fill the body with French knots, using Green Turquoise floss #3849.
4. Outline stitch the wing using Apple Green floss #906.
5. Outline stitch the inside wing lines using Granny Smith Apple floss #907.

Butterflies in the Corners

1. Outline stitch the body outline using Granny Smith Apple floss #907.
2. Satin stitch the eyes using Granny Smith Apple floss #907.
3. Fill the body with French knots using Granny Smith Apple floss #907.
4. Outline stitch the wing outline using Iris Violet floss #3746.
5. Fill the small sections on the wings with French knots using Iris Violet floss #3746.
6. Fill the wings with French knots using Wisteria Violet floss #340.

Butterflies on the Sides

1. Outline stitch the body outline using Apple Green floss #906.
2. Fill the body with French knots using Apple Green floss #906.
3. Outline stitch the wing outline using Wisteria Violet floss #340.
4. Fill the small sections on the wings with French knots using Wisteria Violet floss #340.
5. Fill the rest of the wings with French knots using Iris Violet floss #3746.

Trail

Stitch the trails with French knots using Ecru floss.

Finishing Touches

1. Baste a running stitch along the inside mat line of the stitched piece. This will help guide in the placement on the mat. Wash your stitch piece to remove any dirt and pen markings. See page 10.

2. Use spray adhesive to cover one side of the mat board. Place the batting over the mat and trim the excess from the edges and the center. Center the clean stitched piece over the mat board and trim the excess fabric to ¾" on the outside of the mat. Trim the inside to ¾", clipping corners.
3. Starting in the center, turn the fabric to the back of the mat and tape it in place. Pull the fabric snug and turn the outside edges to the back of the mat and tape them in place. Remove the basting thread. See step photos for mat board frames on page 12.
4. Remove the backing and the glass from the oak frame. Re-assemble with the stitched mat first, followed by the glass, photo, and backing.

4

A home's den is a more relaxed room where the family gathers to watch a good movie or its favorite football team. Fill your den w Americana style accents of red, white, and blue. A "God Bless America" sampler is hung on the wall; an oversized pillow placed on the couch is embellished with an American bald eagle stitched in the center and an accent basket on the table is used to hold mom's threads.

Patriotic Den

God Bless America Sampler

Eagle Pillow

Nantucket Basket

God Bless America Sampler

Add accents of red, white, and blue to your home decor with this God Bless America sampler. Blue, French-knotted stars and red stripes create the border that surrounds "God Bless America." This sampler was stitched on a white even-weave fabric and framed with a navy linen mat and oak frame.

Materials
14" x 18" even-weave needlework fabric
    Winter White* #3865
Pearl cotton balls*, size 8: Dark Polar Blue
    #311, Old Gold #783, Red #321
Embroidery needle
Mat and frame of your choice
Miscellaneous items: tracing paper,
    pencil, light table, disappearing ink
    pen, tape, embroidery hoop, and
    scissors

*Products used: needlework fabric and pearl
cotton by DMC® Corp.

Design Dimensions: 5" x 13"

Instructions

Trace the pattern on pages 108 and 109 onto paper.

Transfer the pattern to the center of the linen fabric. (See page 10.)

Stitch the "God Bless America" pattern using one strand of pearl cotton. Four strands of embroidery floss may be substituted in place of the pearl cotton. Refer to the stitch guide on pages 15 to 19.

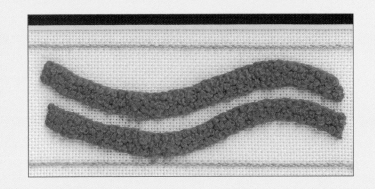

Border

1. Outline stitch the border using Old Gold pearl cotton #783.
2. Outline stitch the stars and fill with French knots using Dark Polar Blue pearl cotton #311.
3. Outline stitch the stripes and fill with French knots using Red pearl cotton #321.

God Bless America

1. Stitch "God Bless" with French knots using Dark Polar Blue pearl cotton #311.
2. Outline stitch "America" using Dark Polar Blue pearl cotton #311.
3. Fill the open areas of "America" with French knots using Red pearl cotton #321.

Finishing Touches

1. Clean the stitched embroidery piece. Refer to page 10.
2. Frame the finished piece. See tips for framing on page 11.

Design Dimensions Eagle: 10" x 7"
Design Dimensions Star: 3½" x 3½"

Eagle Pillow

I once saw an eagle up close at a zoo in South Dakota. His wing was broken and he was being nursed back to health before being released back into the wild. This majestic bird, a national symbol of freedom, has always fascinated and inspired me.

Create this grand 24" square pillow with a French-knotted eagle stitched in the center. Denim fabric surrounds the eagle block and textured stars brighten the corners. Gold tassels are added to the top corners of the pillow.

For an alternate use, the eagle pattern can be used for the center block of a quilt with star blocks added around it.

Materials

14" x 18" ecru-colored even-weave needlework fabric*
6-strand embroidery floss*: Old Gold #783, Red #321, Dark Polar Blue #311, Autumn Gold #3855, Insect Green #3347, one skein; Off White #712 and Hare Brown #840, two skeins; Dark Wood #838 and Root Brown #839, three skeins; White #B5200, four skeins
1½ yd. lightweight denim
24" x 24" pillow insert*
Embroidery needle
Matching sewing thread
2 large gold tassels
Miscellaneous items: sewing machine, tracing paper, pencil, light table, disappearing ink pen, chalk pencil, embroidery hoop, and scissors
Tools: cutting mat, acrylic ruler, and rotary cutter*

Products used: needlework fabric and floss by DMC® Corp., Pop-in-Pillow® insert by Fairfield, and tools by Fiskars®

Instructions

Cut a 13¼" x 11¼" piece from the needlework fabric. With the sewing machine, zigzag the edges of the fabric to prevent unraveling.
Trace the eagle pattern on page 111 onto paper.
Transfer the eagle pattern to the center of the needlework fabric. (See page 10.)
Stitch the eagle pattern. Use four strands of embroidery floss on all stitches. Refer to the stitch guide on pages 15 to 19.

Eagle Head

1. Outline stitch the head, inside lines, and beak using Root Brown floss #839.
2. Stitch one French knot for the center of the eye using Root Brown floss #839.
3. Stitch French knots around the center dot of the eye using Autumn Gold floss #3855.
4. Fill the beak with French knots using Autumn Gold floss #3855.
5. Fill the head with French knots using Off White floss #712.

Shield

1. Outline stitch the shield using Old Gold floss #783.
2. Stitch one row of French knots next to the shield outline using Old Gold floss #783.
3. Fill the top section of the shield with French knots using Dark Polar Blue floss #311.
4. Fill the stripes with French knots using Red floss #321 and White floss #B5200. (See photo for color placement of the stripes.)

Eagle Body

1. Outline stitch the body using Root Brown floss #839.
2. Fill the eagle body and legs with French Knots using Root Brown floss #839.
3. Fill the claws with French knots using Autumn Gold floss #3855.

Tail Feathers

1. Outline stitch each feather and its centerline using Root Brown floss #839.
2. Fill the feathers with French knots using Off White floss #712.

Olive Branch

1. Stem stitch the olive branch stem using Hare Brown floss #840.
2. Lazy daisy stitch the leaves using Insect Green floss #3347.

Spears

1. Outline stitch the staff of the spear using Root Brown floss #839.
2. Fill the spearhead with French knots using Hare Brown floss #840.

Eagle Wing

1. Outline stitch the top feather and center sections using Dark Wood floss #838.
2. Fill the top and center feather sections with French knots using Dark Wood floss #838.
3. Outline stitch the lower feather sections using Root Brown floss #839.
4. Fill the tips of the feathers with French knots using Hare Brown floss #840.
5. Fill the rest of the feathers with French knots using Root Brown floss #839.

Step 6

Completing the Pillow

1. Wash your stitched piece to remove any dirt and pen markings. See page 10 for washing tips.
2. Cut the denim fabric into one 26¼" x 26¼" piece, two 26¼" x 8" pieces, and two 13¼" x 9" pieces.
3. Sew the 13¼" x 9" denim pieces to the top and bottom of the stitched piece using a ⅝" seam allowance. Sew the long strips on the sides. See the pillow instructions on page 13.
4. Trace the star pattern on page 110 four times onto paper and cut out the stars.
5. Pin the star patterns in each corner. This will help you to line up your stars equidistant from each corner.
6. Mark the star pattern with a chalk pencil in each corner. Remove the patterns.
7. Stitch each star with an outline stitch and then fill with French knots using White floss #B5200.

Finishing Touches

Pin and sew a ⅝" seam allowance with the right sides together. Leave a 16" opening on the side. Trim the corners, turn right-side out, and insert the pillow form. See page 13. Close the opening with whipstitches.

Step 7

Design Dimensions: 5" round

Materials

Small covered basket and cushion with 6" design area*
14" x 18" ecru-colored even-weave needlework fabric*
6-strand embroidery floss*: Old Gold #783, Dark Polar
    Blue #311, Fern Green #320
Silk ribbon*: 4mm Quite Blue #585, 4mm Forest Green
    #628, 7mm Red #539
1 yd. gold cord, ¼"
Embroidery needle
8" square of red felt
Miscellaneous items: tracing paper, pencil, light table,
    disappearing ink pen, sewing thread, embroidery hoop,
    and scissors

*Products used: Nantucket Lightship Basket by Sudberry House;
needlework fabric and floss by DMC® Corp.; silk ribbon by
Bucilla® Plaid Enterprises*

Nantucket Basket

Decorate with this American-style pattern
stitched on a small, covered basket.
Silk ribbon is used in the center of the
pattern, surrounded by a navy French-
knotted border. This basket will make a
nice place to tuck away your embroidery
floss for your next project.

Instructions

Trace the pattern on page 114 onto paper.

Transfer the pattern to the center of the fabric. (See page 10.)

Stitch the basket design using four strands of embroidery floss and silk ribbon. Refer to the stitch guide on pages 15 to 19.

Center Pattern

1. Spider web rose stitch the rose using Red 7mm silk ribbon #539.
2. Leaf ribbon stitch the large leaves using Forest Green 4mm silk ribbon #628.
3. Lazy daisy stitch the blue accents using Quite Blue 4mm silk ribbon #585.
4. Stem stitch the stems using Fern Green floss #320.
5. Lazy daisy stitch the small leaves using Forest Green 4mm silk ribbon #628.
6. Lazy daisy stitch the rose buds using Red 7mm silk ribbon #539.
7. Stitch the accents with French knots using Fern Green floss #320.

Border

1. Outline stitch the border using Dark Polar Blue floss #311.
2. Finish stitching the border with French knots using Dark Polar Blue floss #311.

Finishing Touches

1. Wash the embroidered piece. See page 10 for tips.
2. Center the stitched area over the cushion lid that comes with the basket. Trim the fabric within 2" of the edge of the circle cushion.
3. Use heavy thread to sew a running stitch around the edge, ½" from the raw edge. Pull the thread to gather the fabric and secure the thread.
4. Cut a 19½" piece of gold cord and, using the gold embroidery floss, whipstitch it around the circumference of the lid, halfway down the sides of the cushion. This provides a "stop" for

Step 4

the cushion so it does not fall into the basket.

5. Cut two 5" lengths of gold cording. Fold each in half to form a loop and sew one to each side next to the cording. These loops function as lifters for the cushion.

6. To finish the back and cover the gathers and running stitch, cut a circle of felt to fit inside the lid. Glue the felt to the back of the cushion.

Step 5

Step 6

A heart is a symbol of love and romance. For a romantic retreat, create these lovely accent pieces embellished with elegant, stitched hearts. A comfy quilt with heart blocks is waiting to be placed on the bed. A lovely accent pillow for the rocker is adorned with a textured heart and silk ribbon embroidered roses. A bell pull with three stitched hearts cascading down the front is hung nearby. A stitched heart wedding sampler celebrates the beginning of a new love.

5 Romantic He Bedroom

Rose Heart Pillow

Heart Bell Pull

Romantic Heart Quilt

Heart Wedding Sampler

Design Dimensions: 5½" x 6"

Rose Heart Pillow

A lovely accent pillow enhances the rocking chair in our romantic bedroom. A textured, French-knotted heart, with a cluster of silk ribbon roses stitched in the center, embellishes the pillow. Rose-budded vines cascade over the edges of the heart, while a lovely floral print frames the heart block.

Materials

10¼" square of white muslin
½ yd. floral print fabric of your choice
Pearl cotton ball*, size 8: Cream #712
6-strand embroidery floss*: Herb Green #3363
Silk ribbon*: 13mm variegated Ice Cream
   #1308, 13mm variegated Olive Green
   #1311, 7mm Lt. Coral #531, 4mm Pale
   Grass #651
16" x 16" pillow insert*
Embroidery needle
Miscellaneous items: sewing machine, tracing
   paper, pencil, light table, disappearing ink
   pen, embroidery hoop, and scissors
Tools: cutting mat, acrylic ruler, and rotary
   cutter*

*Products used: pearl cotton and floss by DMC®
Corp.; Poly-fil Soft Touch® insert by Fairfield; tools
by Fiskars®*

Instructions

Cut the floral fabric into one 17¼" square, two 5" x 10¼" pieces, and two 5" x 17¼" pieces.
Trace the heart pattern on page 112 onto paper.
Transfer the heart pattern to the center of the white muslin fabric square. (See page 10.)
Stitch the heart pattern using one strand of pearl cotton. Four strands of embroidery floss may be substituted for pearl cotton. Refer to the stitch guide on pages 15 to 19.

Rose Vine

1. Stitch the roses with the spider web rose stitch using Cream pearl cotton #712 and 13mm Ice Cream silk ribbon #1308.
2. Stem stitch the stems using Herb Green floss #3363.
3. Japanese ribbon stitch the large leaves using 7mm Olive Green silk ribbon #1311.
4. Lazy daisy stitch the rose buds using 13mm Ice Cream silk ribbon #1308.
5. Lazy daisy stitch the small buds using 7mm Lt. Coral silk ribbon #531.
6. Lazy daisy stitch the small leaves using 4mm Pale Grass silk ribbon #651.

Heart

1. Outline stitch the heart using Cream pearl cotton #712.
2. Fill the heart with French knots using Cream pearl cotton #712, leaving openings at the bottom of the heart and around the rose vine.

Finishing Touches

1. Wash your stitched piece to remove any dirt and pen markings. See page 10 for tips.
2. Sew the floral fabric to the needlework square using ⅝" seams. Pin and sew the short strips to the top and bottom of the heart square. Press the seams open. Pin and sew the long strips on the sides of the center piece. Press the seam toward the outside edge. See page 13.

3. Pin the pillow back to the pillow front with right sides together. Sew a ⅝" seam allowance, leaving an 8" opening on one side for turning. Trim the excess fabric from the corners. Turn right-side out. Insert the pillow form. Close the pillow opening with whipstitches. Refer to the pillow steps on page 13.

Materials

½ yd. rose floral print fabric

¼ yd. cream-colored fabric

Pearl cotton balls*, size 8: China Red #304,
Dark Raspberry Rose #309, Dark Rose
#335

7" brass bell pull hardware*

Embroidery needle

Miscellaneous items: sewing machine, tracing
paper, pencil, light table, disappearing ink
pen, embroidery hoop, and scissors

Tools: cutting mat, acrylic ruler, and rotary
cutter*

*Products used: pearl cotton by DMC® Corp.; bell
pull hardware by Wichelt Imports; tools by Fiskars®

Heart Bell Pull

For a lovely accent, hang the finished bell pull next to your bed. A repeated pattern of three hearts stitched in different shades, from red to rose, make up this bell pull pattern. The hearts are stitched on a cream-colored background fabric and surrounded by a rosy floral print. The fabric is mounted with gold heart-scrolled hardware.

Design Dimensions: 3¼" x 3¼"

Instructions

Cut one 6¼" x 13¾" rectangle of cream-colored fabric.
Cut two 5½" x 6¼" pieces of floral fabric and one 9¾" x 21" piece.
Trace the heart pattern on page 113 onto paper.
Transfer the heart pattern to the center of the cream-colored fabric. (See page 10.)
Stitch the heart pattern using one strand of pearl cotton. Four strands of embroidery floss may be substituted for pearl cotton. Refer to the stitch guide on pages 15 to 19.

Hearts

Outline stitch each heart and fill the sections with French knots.
1. Stitch the top heart using China Red pearl cotton #304.
2. Stitch the center heart using Dark Raspberry Rose pearl cotton #309.
3. Stitch the bottom heart using Dark Rose pearl cotton #335.

Step 3

Finishing Touches

1. Wash your stitched piece to remove any dirt and pen markings. See page 10 for washing instructions.
2. Sew the floral fabric to the needlework strip using ⅝" seams. Pin and sew the short strips to the top and bottom of the heart strip. Press the seams open. Pin and sew the long strip to one side of this.
3. Join the two long sides, right sides together. Pin the edges together and sew with a ⅝" seam allowance. Press the seam open. This will form a tube.
4. Turn the tube right-side out. Center the stitching and press the sides.
5. Slip 1½" of one fabric end through the bell pull hardware. Turn the raw edges under ½" and whipstitch along the edge. Repeat with the other end.

Step 5

Design Dimensions: 5" x 5"

Romantic Heart Quilt

The bed is draped with a romantic quilt full of easy-to-stitch heart blocks arranged in a heart-shaped pattern. The blocks are stitched on a flesh-colored background fabric and vary in shades from red to pale rose. They are surrounded by a deep rose floral print.

Materials

2¾ yd. deep rose floral print in extra wide (90") width

2½ yd. white muslin in extra wide (90") width for the backing

1¼ yd. flesh-colored fabric; 45" width

Queen size high loft batting*

Pearl cotton balls*, size 8: Dark Red #498, Dark Raspberry Rose #309, Dark Rose #335, Medium Rose #899, Grenadine Pink #760

Embroidery needle

Matching sewing thread

Miscellaneous items: sewing machine, tracing paper, pencil, light table, disappearing ink pen, embroidery hoop, and scissors

Tools: cutting mat, acrylic ruler, and rotary cutter*

Products used: pearl cotton by DMC® Corp.; Poly-fil® batting by Fairfield; tools by Fiskars®

Instructions

Cut sixteen 8½" squares from the flesh-colored fabric to use for the stitched blocks.

Trace the heart pattern on page 114 onto paper.

Transfer the heart pattern to the center of the fabric squares. (See page 10.)

Stitch the heart pattern using one strand of pearl cotton. Four strands of embroidery floss may be substituted for pearl cotton. Refer to the stitch guide on pages 15 to 19.

Heart Blocks

Stitch all the hearts with French knots.

1. Stitch two blocks using Dark Red pearl cotton #498.
2. Stitch two blocks using Grenadine Pink pearl cotton #760.
3. Stitch four blocks using Dark Raspberry Rose pearl cotton #309.
4. Stitch four blocks using Dark Rose pearl cotton #335.
5. Stitch four blocks using Medium Rose pearl cotton #899.

Fabric Blocks

Cut the floral fabric into the following pieces:

Two 84½" x 8½"
Two 72½" x 14½"
Two 32½" x 8½"
One 40½" x 8½"
Six 24½" x 8½"
Four 16½" x 8½"
Eight 8½" x 8½"

1. Sew the quilt blocks together using a ¼" seam allowance. Refer to the quilt block layout for placement of the pieces. (See page 73.)
2. Sew one row of blocks at a time and press the seams open.
3. Sew the rows together.
4. Sew the top and bottom band pieces on first, then the side band pieces.

Finishing Touches

1. Spread the quilt batting out on a clean floor. Spread the finished quilt top over the batting. Randomly pin the top to the batting.

2. Baste the quilt top edges to the batting with a long running stitch. Trim away any excess batting.
3. Press the backing fabric and spread it over the quilt top, right sides together. Pin around the edges and trim the excess fabric from the edge of the quilt.
4. Sew the layers together using a ⅝" seam allowance. Leave a 36" opening on one edge. Trim the corners and turn right-side out. Close the opening using whipstitches.

5. Spread the finished quilt out on the floor again. Smooth and pin the layers together, starting in the center and working out toward the edges.
6. Tie the quilt using Grenadine Pink pearl cotton #760. Place a tie on each corner of the stitched blocks but not in the stitched blocks. Also place ties every 4" to 6" on the floral print. Refer to page 14 for more information on tying quilts.

The finished quilt measures approximately 84" x 88".

Quilt Block Layout

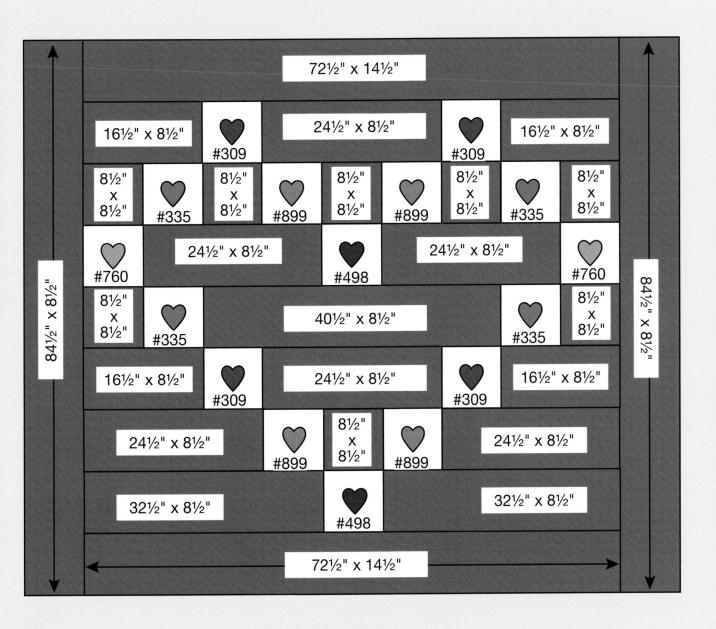

Design Dimensions: 5½" x 6"

Heart Wedding Sampler

Commemorate that special day when two young hearts became one in marriage with this lovely wedding sampler. The sampler has a simple French-knotted border that divides the sampler into three sections. The top section of the sampler holds a vine of roses stitched with silk ribbon. The center section is a heart with roses surrounding the young couple's names. The lower section of the sampler, reminding us of that special date, is accented on both sides with more rose vines.

Materials

14" x 18" ecru even-weave
    needlework fabric*
6-strand embroidery floss*: Deer
    Brown #841, two skeins
Silk ribbon*: 4mm Olive #509, 4mm
    Banana #502, 4mm Jungle Green
    #653, 2 cards each; variegated
    7mm Burgundies #7115, 3 cards
Embroidery needle
Frame and mat of your choice
Foam core board
Miscellaneous items: tracing paper,
    pencil, light table, disappearing
    ink pen, embroidery hoop, and
    scissors

*Products used: floss and needlework
fabric by DMC® Corp.; silk ribbon by
Bucilla® Plaid Enterprises*

Instructions

Trace the sampler pattern on page 115 onto paper. Trace the appropriate names and date from the letters and numbers, page 110.
Transfer the sampler pattern to the center of the needlework fabric square. (See page 10.)
Stitch the heart pattern using four strands of floss. Refer to the stitch guide, pages 15 to 19.

Sampler

1. Stitch the border with French knots using Deer Brown floss #841.
2. Stem stitch the vines using Deer Brown floss #841.
3. Spider web rose stitch the roses using Deer Brown floss #841 and variegated Burgundies silk ribbon #7115.
4. Lazy daisy stitch the leaves using Jungle Green silk ribbon #653.
5. Stitch the small flowers with French knots using Banana silk ribbon #502.
6. Stitch the clusters with French knots using Olive silk ribbon #509.
7. Stitch the heart outline with outline stitch and French knots using Deer Brown floss #841.
8. Outline stitch the lettering and numbers using Deer Brown floss #841.

Finishing Touches

1. Wash your stitched piece to remove any dirt and pen markings. See page 10.
2. Center the embroidered piece over the mounting board and pull the excess fabric to the back, taping it in place.
3. Frame the mounted piece with mat board and the frame of your choice. See page 11.

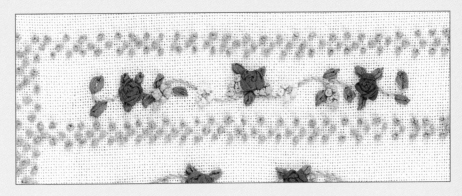

6 Vintage Guest Room

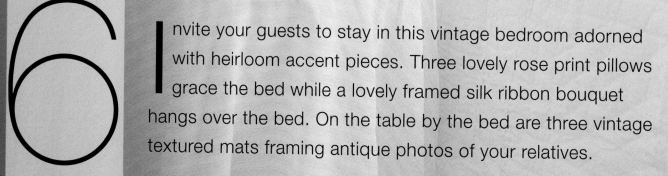

nvite your guests to stay in this vintage bedroom adorned with heirloom accent pieces. Three lovely rose print pillows grace the bed while a lovely framed silk ribbon bouquet hangs over the bed. On the table by the bed are three vintage textured mats framing antique photos of your relatives.

Three Vintage Pillows

Three Vintage Frames

Oval Framed Bouquet

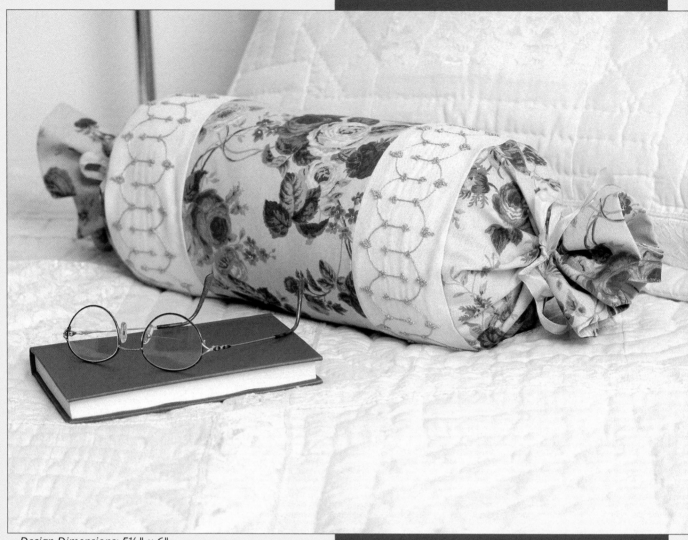

Design Dimensions: 5½" x 6"

Neck Pillow

Relax with a good book and this comfy, floral-printed neck pillow, which is embellished on both ends with candlewick stitching. An antique fence inspired this pattern.

Materials

14" x 5" neck pillow
½ yd. rose floral fabric
¼ yd. cream fabric
Pearl cotton ball*, size 8: Dawn Rose #758
Embroidery needle
1½ yd. wired-edge ivory ribbon, ½"
Two rubber bands
Miscellaneous items: sewing machine, tracing paper, pencil, light table, white sewing thread, disappearing ink pen, embroidery hoop, and scissors
Tools: cutting mat, acrylic ruler, and rotary cutter*

Products used: pearl cotton by DMC® Corp.; Poly-fil Soft Touch® insert by Fairfield; tools by Fiskars®

Instructions

Cut the cream fabric into two 4¾" x 20½" strips.

Trace the neck pillow pattern on page 116 onto paper.

Transfer the neck pillow pattern; center the pattern ¾" from one end of the strip. To finish transferring the pattern, slide the fabric strip down the pattern, overlapping the traced pattern. Continue tracing the pattern to the end of the fabric strip. (See page 10.)

Stitch the neck pillow pattern using one strand of pearl cotton. Four strands of embroidery floss may be substituted for pearl cotton. Refer to the stitch guide on pages 15 to 19.

Neck Pillow

1. Outline stitch the pattern using Dawn Rose pearl cotton #758.
2. Stitch the clusters with French knots using Dawn Rose pearl cotton #758.
3. Repeat with each strip.

Finishing Touches

1. Wash your stitched piece to remove any dirt and pen markings. See page 10.
2. Cut the rose floral fabric into two 10" x 20½" pieces for the end fabric strips. Cut one 8¼" x 20½" piece for the center fabric strip.
3. All seams use a ⅝" seam allowance. Alternate the embroidered strips with the fabric strip: floral end, embroidered, center, embroidered, floral end. Press the seams open.
4. Turn each end down ½"; press, and turn down 2" more to create a hem. Sew along the edge to secure the hem.
5. Line up the seams and pin the long sides together; sew the long seam.
6. Turn the fabric right-side out. Insert the pillow form into the center of the pillow tube. On each end, gather up the fabric next to the pillow form and wrap a rubber band around the fabric. Cut the ivory wired ribbon in half and tie a bow on each end.

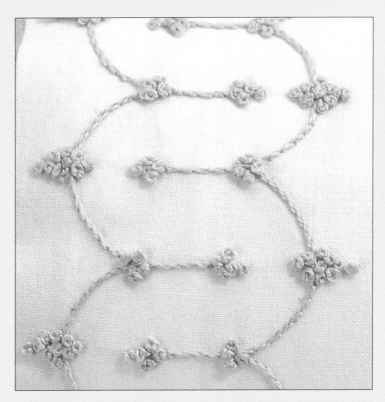

Steps 3-5

Step 6

Design Dimensions: 3¼" x 3¼"

Square Pillow

A Dawn Rose French-knotted pattern surrounds a silk ribbon rose which mimics the look of chenille. Red French knot clusters and dark green leaves accent the rose. A lovely floral print surrounds the stitched panel.

Materials

14" square pillow insert
½ yd. rose floral fabric
6¼" square cream-colored fabric
Pearl cotton ball*, size 8: Dawn Rose #758
6-strand floss*: Brown Red #355
Silk ribbon*: 7mm variegated Candlelight #7101; 7mm variegated Jungle Green #7102
Embroidery needle
Miscellaneous items: sewing machine, tracing paper, pencil, light table, white sewing thread, disappearing ink pen, embroidery hoop, and scissors
Tools: cutting mat, acrylic ruler, and rotary cutter*

Products used: pearl cotton and floss by DMC® Corp.; Poly-fil Soft Touch® insert by Fairfield; silk ribbon by Bucilla® Plaid Enterprises; tools by Fiskars®

Instructions

Trace the square pillow pattern on page 118 onto paper.

Transfer the pattern to the center of the cream-colored fabric square. (See page 10.)

Stitch the pillow pattern using one strand of pearl cotton. Four strands of embroidery floss may be substituted for the pearl cotton. Use embroidery floss for the red cluster and silk ribbon for the rose. Refer to the stitch guide on pages 15 to 19.

Square Pillow

1. Spider web rose stitch the rose using Dawn Rose pearl cotton #758 and 7mm Candlelight silk ribbon #7101.
2. Lazy daisy stitch the leaves using 7mm Jungle Green silk ribbon #7102.
3. Stitch the red clusters with French knots using Brown Red floss #355.
4. Stitch the pattern with French knots using Dawn Rose pearl cotton #758.

Finishing Touches

1. Wash your stitched piece to remove any dirt and pen markings. See page 10.
2. Cut the rose floral fabric into two 5¾" x 15¼" pieces, two 6¼" x 5¾" pieces, and one 15¼" square.
3. Sew the floral fabric to the needlework square using ⅝" seams. Pin and sew the short strips to the top and bottom of the center square. Press the seams open. Pin and sew the long strips on the sides of the center piece. Press the seams open. See page 13.
4. Pin the pillow back to the pillow front, with right sides together. Sew a ⅝" seam allowance leaving an 8" opening on one side for turning. Trim the excess fabric from the corners. Turn right-side out. Insert the pillow form. Close the pillow opening with whipstitches. See pillow steps on page 13.

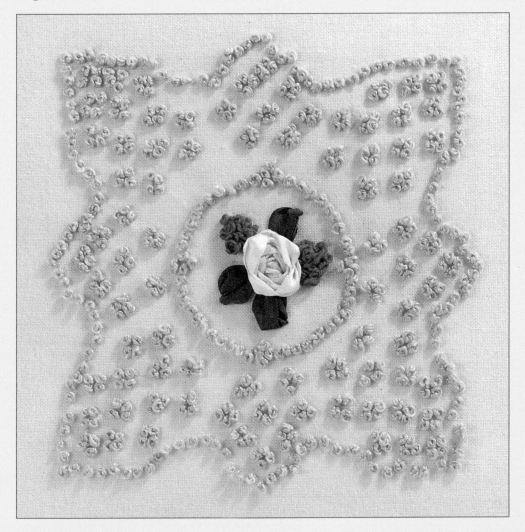

Design Dimensions: 5" x 5"

Envelope Pillow

This lovely envelope pillow is adorned with a vintage-style, stitched, oval frame. An elegant bouquet is showcased inside the stitched frame. Attach a vintage button to the bottom of the flap for an elegant touch.

Materials

12" x 16" pillow insert*

½ yd. rose floral printed fabric

12½" square of cream-colored fabric

Pearl cotton ball*, size 8: Dawn Rose #758

6-strand floss*: Earth Gray #642

Silk ribbon*: 4mm Deep Red #536, 4mm Olive #509, 7mm variegated Candlelight #7101, 7mm variegated Jungle Green #7102

Embroidery needle

One antique button

Miscellaneous items: sewing machine, tracing paper, pencil, light table, disappearing ink pen, embroidery hoop, and scissors

Tools: cutting mat, acrylic ruler, and rotary cutter*

Products used: pearl cotton and floss by DMC® Corp.; Poly-fil Soft Touch® insert by Fairfield; silk ribbon by Bucilla® Plaid Enterprises; tools by Fiskars®

Instructions

Cut the cream fabric square across its diagonal to make two triangles. Cut two rose floral rectangles, 13¼" x 17¼". (See page 9.)

Trace the rectangle pillow pattern on page 117 onto paper.

Transfer the pattern to the center of one of the triangles. (See page 10.)

Stitch the pattern using one strand of pearl cotton. Four strands of embroidery floss may be substituted for the pearl cotton. Refer to the stitch guide on pages 15 to 19.

Envelope Pillow

1. Stitch the border with French knots using Dawn Rose pearl cotton #758.
2. Stem stitch the stems using Earth Gray floss #642.
3. Spider web rose stitch the red roses using Earth Gray floss #642 and 4mm Deep Red silk ribbon #536.
4. Lazy daisy stitch the buds using Deep Red silk ribbon #536.
5. Spider web rose stitch the white roses using Earth Gray floss #642 and 7mm Candlelight #7101.
6. Japanese ribbon stitch the small leaves using 4mm Olive silk ribbon #509.
7. Lazy daisy stitch the large leaves using 7mm Jungle Green silk ribbon #7102.

Finishing Touches

1. Wash your stitched piece to remove any dirt and pen markings. See page 10.
2. With right sides together, sew the triangle pieces along the short sides. Trim the corners and turn right-side out. Press the edges.
3. Pin and hand baste the triangle to one of the rectangle floral fabric pieces.
4. With right sides together, place the other rectangular floral fabric piece on top. Leave an 8" opening on the bottom edge and sew the pillow together using a ⅝" seam allowance.
5. Insert the pillow form and close the opening using whipstitches. Attach the button at the bottom of the triangle flap. See page 13.

Step 3

Design Dimensions: 6" x 4", 5¼" x 3½", 6¼" x 4¼"

Three Vintage Frames

Three generations of mothers are displayed in these simple, vintage-style, photo mat frames. The photos are pictures of my mother, grandmother, and great grandmother. I enjoy creating ways to display memorabilia of the special people who have touched my life.

Materials

Two 5" x 7" photo mats with 3" x 5" oval openings
One 5" x 7" photo mat with a 1½" x 2½" opening
Three photo frames of your choice
¼ yd. beige fabric
Pearl cotton balls*, size 8: Antique Lilac #315 and Garnet Red #902
Embroidery needle
Miscellaneous items: tracing paper, pencil, light table, disappearing ink pen, tape, embroidery hoop, and scissors
Tools: cutting mat, acrylic ruler, and rotary cutter*

Products used: pearl cotton by DMC® Corp.; tools by Fiskars®

Instructions

Cut three 9" x 7" pieces of beige fabric.

Trace the mat patterns on pages 119 to 121 onto paper.

Transfer the pattern to the center of the fabric. (See page 10.)

Stitch each mat pattern using one strand of pearl cotton. Four strands of embroidery floss may be substituted for the pearl cotton. Refer to the stitch guide on pages 15 to 19.

Stitch a long stitch around each mat opening. (See page 12.)

Frames

1. Outline stitch the outlines using Antique Lilac pearl cotton #315.
2. Stitch all the French knots using Garnet Red pearl cotton #902.

Finishing Touches

1. Baste a running stitch along the inside mat line of the stitched piece. This will help guide in the placement on the mat.
2. Wash your stitched piece to remove any dirt and pen markings. See page 10 for washing tips.
3. Center the stitched piece over the mat board and trim the excess fabric to ¾" on the outside of the mat. Trim the inside to ¾", clipping the corners of the curves.
4. Starting in the center, pull the fabric to the back of the mat and tape it in place. Pull the fabric snug and turn the outside edges to the back of the mat, taping them in place.
5. Remove the basting thread. See the directions for mats on page 12.
6. Assemble the frame with the stitched mat first, followed by the glass, the photo, and the backing.

Design Dimensions: 8½" x 6½"

Oval Framed Bouquet

An elegant vintage ribbon rose bouquet surrounded by a candlewick border rests on the dresser. Our bouquet is adorned with ivory and pink variegated roses. Accent flowers of pale yellow and off-white are nestled among the roses. A gold oval frame surrounds the array.

Materials

14" x 18" piece of 28-ct. cream-colored linen*
Pearl cotton ball*, size 8: Ecru
6-strand embroidery floss*: Deer Brown #841
Silk ribbon*: 13mm variegated Olive Green #1311, 13mm Ivory #1321, 7mm variegated Terra Cotta #7110, 4mm Off-White #501, 4mm Olive #509, 4mm Pale Grass #651, and 4mm Creamy Yellow #655
Embroidery needle
Batting
Mounting board
Oval frame
Miscellaneous items: tracing paper, pencil, light table, disappearing ink pen, tape, embroidery hoop, and scissors

Products used: pearl cotton and floss by DMC® Corp.; silk ribbon by Bucilla® Plaid Enterprises; linen by Charles Craft®

Instructions

Trace the oval frame pattern on page 122 onto paper.

Transfer the pattern to the center of the fabric. (See page 10.)

Stitch the pattern using one strand of pearl cotton. Four strands of embroidery floss may be substituted for the pearl cotton. Refer to the stitch guide on pages 15 to 19.

Border

1. Outline stitch the border using Ecru pearl cotton.
2. Stitch the French knots along the outside edge of the border using Ecru pearl cotton.

Silk Ribbon Bouquet

1. Stem stitch the stems using Deer Brown floss #841.
2. Stitch the clusters on the stems with French knots using 4mm Off White silk ribbon #501.
3. Spider web rose stitch the pink roses using Ecru pearl cotton and 7mm variegated Terra Cotta silk ribbon #7110.
4. Spider web rose stitch the white roses using Ecru pearl cotton and 13mm Ivory silk ribbon #1321.
5. Lazy daisy stitch the rose buds using 7mm variegated Terra Cotta silk ribbon #7110.
6. Stitch the clusters with French knots using 4mm Creamy Yellow silk ribbon #655.
7. Lazy daisy stitch the large leaves using 13mm variegated Olive Green silk ribbon #1311.
8. Lazy daisy stitch the medium-sized leaves using 4mm Pale Grass silk ribbon #651.
9. Japanese ribbon stitch the small leaves using 4mm Olive silk ribbon #509.

Finishing Touches

1. Wash your stitched piece to remove any dirt and pen markings. See page 10.
2. Trace the opening of the oval frame onto the mounting board and cut it out.
3. Place the batting on top of the mounting board. Center the stitching over the batting.
4. Trim the fabric within 2" of the mounting board edge. With heavy thread, sew a running stitch ½" from the raw edge. Pull the thread to gather the fabric around the mounting board. Secure the stitches.
5. Place the needlework board in the frame and tape it to the back of the frame. Cover the back with paper. See page 11 for framing tips.

The Nursery

7

A home's nursery is a special place for those new little people in your life. Celebrate the birth of that little boy or girl with a sampler. Keep them warm with a flannel blanket sporting three little ducklings. While the little one is sleeping, hang a lovely little "baby sleeping" pillow on the doorknob.

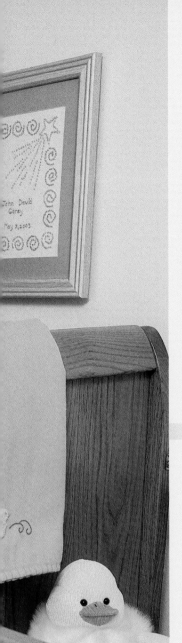

Baby Girl Sampler

Baby Boy Sampler

Duck Blanket

Baby Sleeping Pillow

Design Dimensions: 7" x 9"

Baby Girl Sampler

A repeated heart-shaped pattern with small silk ribbon roses creates the border for this baby girl's sampler. The name is surrounded with a textured border and, for an elegant touch, a vine with roses is added below the name box.

Materials

14" x 18" piece of 25-ct. even-weave fabric, Winter White #3865*

Pearl cotton balls*, size 8: Lettuce Head Green #3348, Rosebud Pink #605, and Hyacinth Pink #604

Silk ribbon*: 4mm Olive #509 and #4mm Lt. Pink #544

Embroidery needle

Frame and mat of your choice

14" x 16" piece of green check fabric

Spray adhesive

Foam core board

Miscellaneous items: tracing paper, pencil, light table, disappearing ink pen, embroidery hoop, and scissors

Products used: even-weave fabric and pearl cotton by DMC® Corp.; silk ribbon by Bucilla® Plaid Enterprises

Instructions

Trace the sampler pattern on page 123 onto paper. To make the names and date, trace the appropriate letters and numbers from page 110. *Transfer* the sampler pattern to the center of the needlework fabric. (See page 10.)

Stitch the sampler pattern using one strand of pearl cotton. Four strands of embroidery floss may be substituted for pearl cotton. Refer to the stitch guide on pages 15 to 19.

Heart Border

1. Stitch the heart border with French knots using Rosebud Pink pearl cotton #605.
2. Stitch the clusters with French knots using Hyacinth Pink pearl cotton #604.
3. Lazy daisy stitch the small rose leaves using Lettuce Head Green pearl cotton #3348.
4. Stitch the small roses with French knots using 4mm Lt. Pink silk ribbon #544.

Name Block

1. Stitch the border clusters with French knots using Hyacinth Pink pearl cotton #604.
2. Lazy daisy stitch the rose leaves using Olive silk ribbon #509.
3. Spider web rose stitch the roses using Rosebud Pink pearl cotton #605 and Lt. Pink silk ribbon #544.
4. Outline stitch the lettering and date using Rosebud Pink pearl cotton #605.

Rose Vine

1. Spider web rose stitch the roses using Rosebud Pink pearl cotton #605 and Lt. Pink silk ribbon #544.
2. Lazy daisy stitch the leaves using Olive silk ribbon #509.
3. Stitch the clusters with French knots using Hyacinth Pink pearl cotton #604.

Finishing Touches

1. Wash your stitched piece to remove any dirt and pen markings. See page 10.
2. Center the embroidery piece over the mounting board and pull the excess fabric to the back, taping it in place.

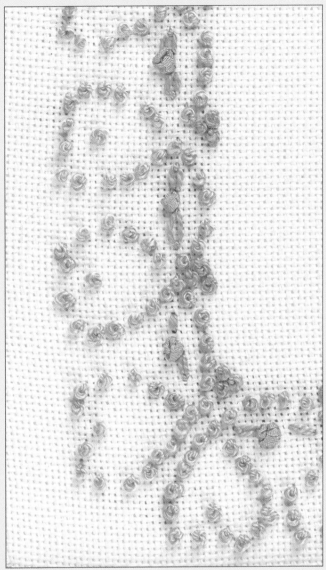

3. Spray adhesive on the front of the mat board. Cover the mat board with the green check fabric. Trim the excess fabric to ½" from the edges of the mat board. Turn the fabric to the back and tape it in place. See page 12.
4. Frame the mounted piece with the frame of your choice. See page 11 for framing tips.

Design Dimensions: 7" x 9"

Baby Boy Sampler

Surrounded by a border of celery and light green swirls, the star shines bright in the corner of this little boy's sampler.

Materials

14" x 18" piece of 25-ct. even-weave fabric, Winter White #3865*

Pearl cotton balls*, size 8: Celery Green #772, Light Green #504, and Sea Mist Blue #747

Embroidery needle

Frame and mat of your choice

Foam core board

Miscellaneous items: tracing paper, pencil, light table, disappearing ink pen, embroidery hoop, and scissors

*Products used: even-weave fabric and pearl cotton by DMC® Corp.

Instructions

Trace the sampler pattern on page 124 onto paper. To make the names and date, trace the appropriate letters and numbers from page 110. *Transfer* the sampler pattern to the center of the fabric. (See page 10.)

Stitch the sampler pattern using one strand of pearl cotton. Four strands of embroidery floss may be substituted for pearl cotton. Refer to the stitch guide on pages 15 to 19.

Star and Border

1. Stitch the star with French knots using Sea Mist Blue pearl cotton #747.
2. Stitch every other swirl with French knots using Light Green pearl cotton #504.

3. Stitch every other swirl with French knots using Celery Green pearl cotton # 772.
4. Outline stitch the lettering and date using Light Green pearl cotton #504.

Finishing Touches

1. Wash your stitched piece to remove any dirt and pen markings. See page 10.
2. Press the backside of the stitched piece. Center the embroidery piece over the mounting board and pull the excess fabric to the back, taping it in place.
3. Frame the mounted piece with the mat board and frame of your choice. See page 11 for framing tips.

Design Dimensions: 9¼" x 1½"

Duck Blanket

Three little yellow ducklings with blue swirls of water make up this simple border pattern stitched on one edge of seafoam green flannel. The crib-sized blanket is tied with seafoam green pearl cotton threads. Blue buttonhole stitches line the edge of the blanket. The finished blanket is 32" x 42".

Materials

2 yd. seafoam green flannel
Crib size batting*
Pearl cotton balls*, size 8: Grapefruit Yellow #744, Delft Blue #322, Light Green #504, and Curry Yellow #972
Embroidery needle
Matching sewing thread
Miscellaneous items: sewing machine, tracing paper, pencil, light table, disappearing ink pen, embroidery hoop, and scissors
Tools: cutting mat, acrylic ruler, and rotary cutter*

*Products used: pearl cotton by DMC® Corp.; Poly-fil® batting by Fairfield; tools by Fiskars®

Instructions

Trace the duck pattern on page 116 onto paper.

Transfer the duck pattern, centering it 2" from the bottom edge of one flannel fabric piece. (See page 10.)

Stitch the duck pattern using one strand of pearl cotton. Four strands of embroidery floss may be substituted for pearl cotton. Refer to the stitch guide on pages 15 to 19.

Duck

1. Outline stitch the outline using Grapefruit Yellow pearl cotton #744.
2. Stitch the ducks' beaks with French knots using Curry Yellow pearl cotton #972.
3. Stitch the ducks' eyes with French knots using Curry Yellow pearl cotton #972.
4. Fill the ducks with French knots using Grapefruit Yellow pearl cotton #744.
5. Outline stitch the waves using Delft Blue pearl cotton #322.

Finishing Touches

1. Spread the quilt batting out on a clean floor. Spread the finished quilt top over the batting. Randomly pin the top to the batting.
2. Baste the top to the batting around the edges with a long running stitch. Trim any excess batting away.
3. Press the backing fabric and spread it over the quilt top, right sides together. Pin around the edges and trim away the excess fabric from the edge of the quilt.
4. Sew the layers together using a ⅝" seam allowance. Leave an 18" opening on one edge.

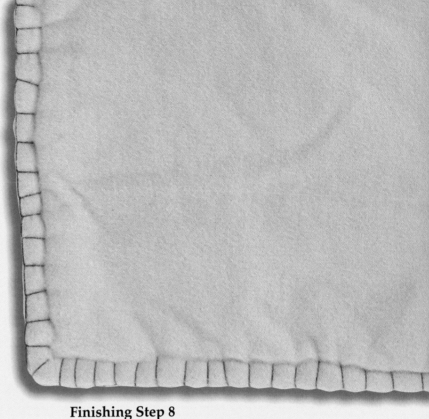

Finishing Step 8

5. Trim the corners and turn the quilt right-side out. Close the opening with whipstitches.
6. Spread the finished quilt out on the floor again. Starting in the center, work out toward the edges, smoothing and pinning the layers together.
7. Tie the quilt every 4" to 6" using Light Green pearl cotton #504. Refer to the quilt technique section on page 14.
8. Stitch the edges of the blanket with buttonhole stitches using Delft Blue pearl cotton #322. See page 16.

The finished quilt measures approximately 32" x 42".

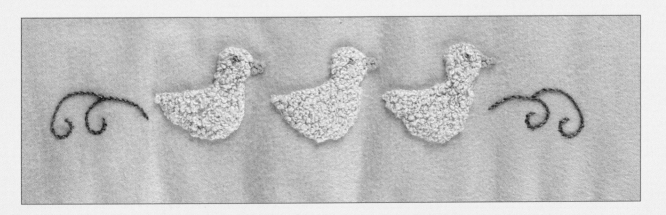

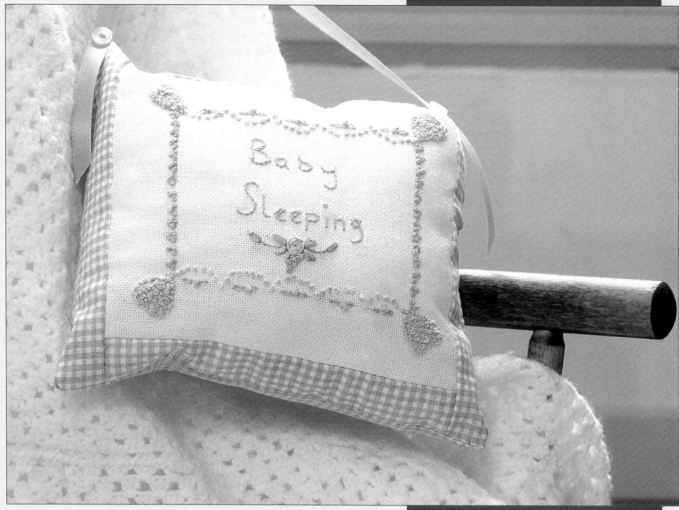

Design Dimensions: 5½" x 4¾"

Baby Sleeping Pillow

Do not disturb … the baby is sleeping. Create this lovely "baby sleeping" pillow to hang on the doorknob of the baby's room. Hearts adorn the corners of the pattern with rose buds, and French knots create the border. "Baby sleeping" is stitched with outline stitches and a simple ribbon rose accents the pillow. Green and white check fabric surrounds the stitching. Use buttons to attach the ribbon for hanging.

Materials

14" x 18" piece of 25-ct. even-weave needlework fabric Winter White #3865*

¼ yd. green check fabric

Poly-fil fiberfill*

Pearl cotton balls*, size 8: Lettuce Head Green #3348, Rosebud Pink #605, and Hyacinth Pink #604

Silk ribbon*: 4mm Olive #509 and #4mm Lt. Pink #544

Embroidery needle

18" pink double-faced satin ribbon

2 small pearl buttons

Miscellaneous items: sewing machine, tracing paper, pencil, light table, disappearing ink pen, embroidery hoop, and scissors

Tools: cutting mat, acrylic ruler, and rotary cutter*

*Products used: needlework fabric and pearl cotton by DMC® Corp.; silk ribbon by Bucilla® Plaid Enterprises; Soft Touch Poly-fil® by Fairfield; tools by Fiskars®

Instructions

Cut the even-weave fabric into a 6" x 7" piece. From the green check fabric, cut two 1½" x 7" strips, two 8½" x 1½" strips, and one 8½" square.

Trace the pattern on page 125 onto paper.

Transfer the pattern to the center of the needlework fabric. (See page 10.)

Stitch the baby sleeping pattern using one strand of pearl cotton. Four strands of embroidery floss may be substituted for pearl cotton. Refer to the stitch guide on pages 15 to 19.

Heart Border

1. Outline stitch the hearts and fill them with French knots using Rosebud Pink pearl cotton #605.
2. Stitch the border with French knots using Hyacinth Pink pearl cotton #604.
3. Lazy daisy stitch the small rose leaves using Lettuce Head Green pearl cotton #3348.
4. Stitch the small roses with French knots using 4mm Lt. Pink silk ribbon #544.

Baby Sleeping

1. Outline stitch the lettering using Hyacinth Pink pearl cotton #604.
2. Stem stitch the stems using Lettuce Head Green pearl cotton #3348.
3. Lazy daisy stitch the leaves using Olive silk ribbon #509.
4. Spider web rose stitch the roses using Rosebud Pink pearl cotton #605 and Lt. Pink silk ribbon #544.
5. Stitch the clusters with French knots using Hyacinth Pink pearl cotton #604.

Finishing Touches

1. Wash your stitched piece to remove any dirt and pen markings. See page 10.
2. Sew the check fabric to the needlework square using ⅝" seams. Pin and sew the short strips to the top and bottom of the stitched block. Press the seams open. Pin and sew the long strips on the sides of the center piece. Press the seams open. See page 13.
3. Pin the pillow back to the pillow front, right sides together. Sew a ⅝" seam allowance leaving a 4" opening on one side for turning.
4. Trim the excess fabric from the corners. Turn right-side out. Fill the pillow with fiberfill. Close the pillow opening using whipstitches. See pillow steps on page 13.
5. Attach the ribbon with buttons on the top corners of the pillow.

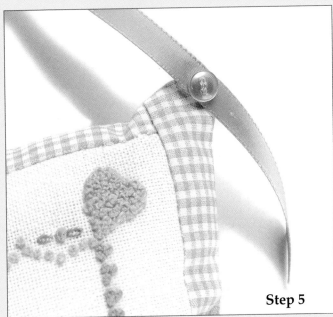

Step 5

Patterns

Hydrangea Mirror (see page 26)

Vine Clock (see page 24)

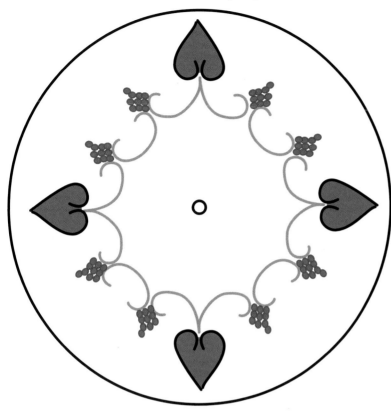

English Ivy Keepsake Box
(see page 28)

Welcome Sign (see page 22)

Strawberry Recipe Box (see page 32)

Strawberry Dishtowel and Frame (see page 34)

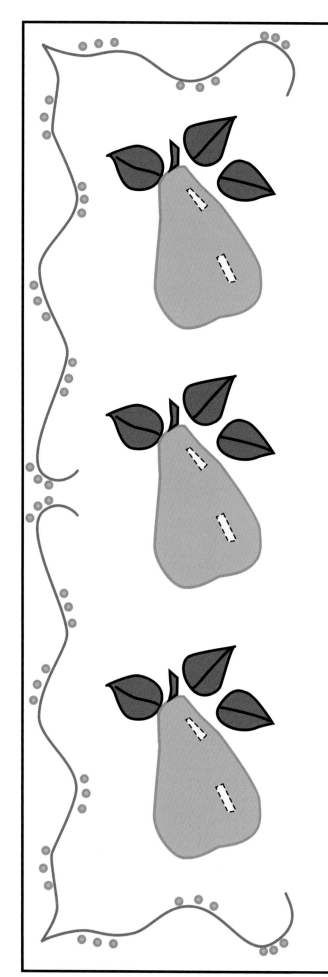

Pear Place Mat and Napkin Set
(see page 36)

Butterfly Pillow (see page 45)

Dragonfly Pillow (see page 42)

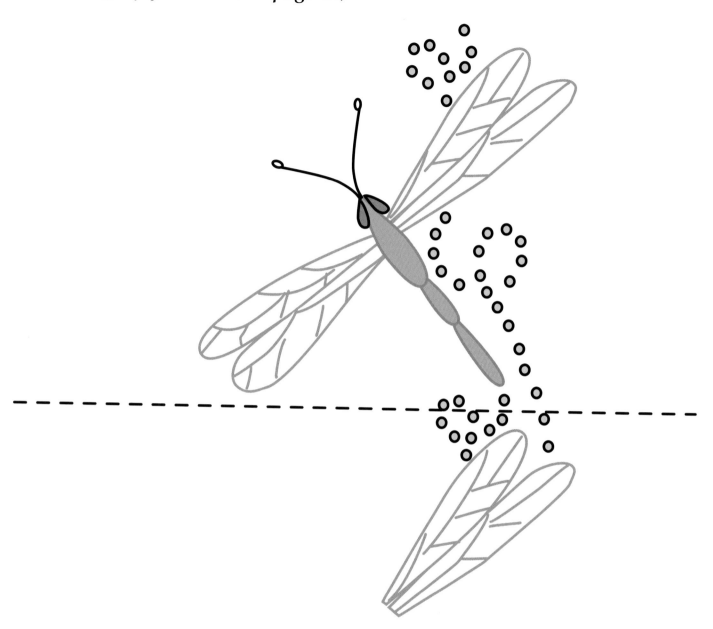

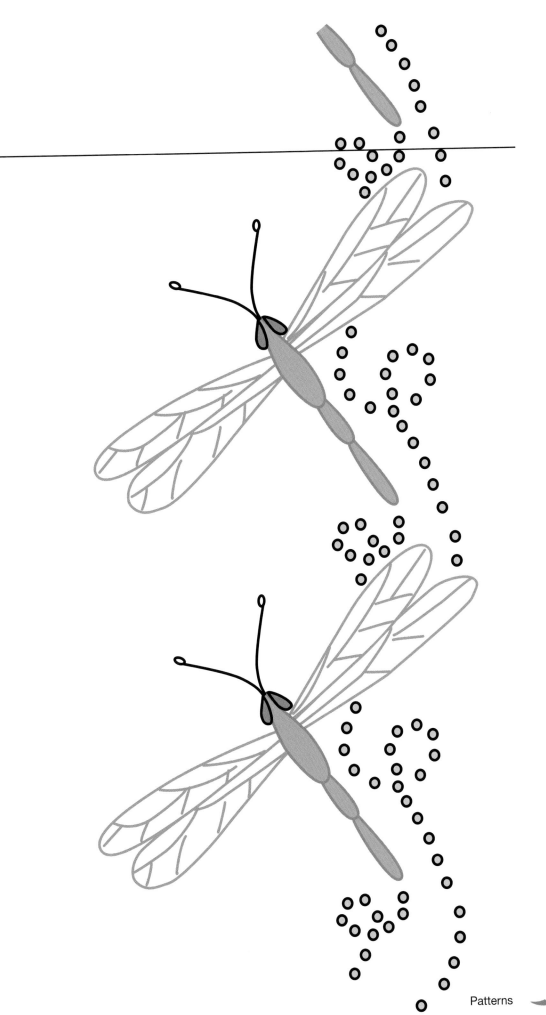

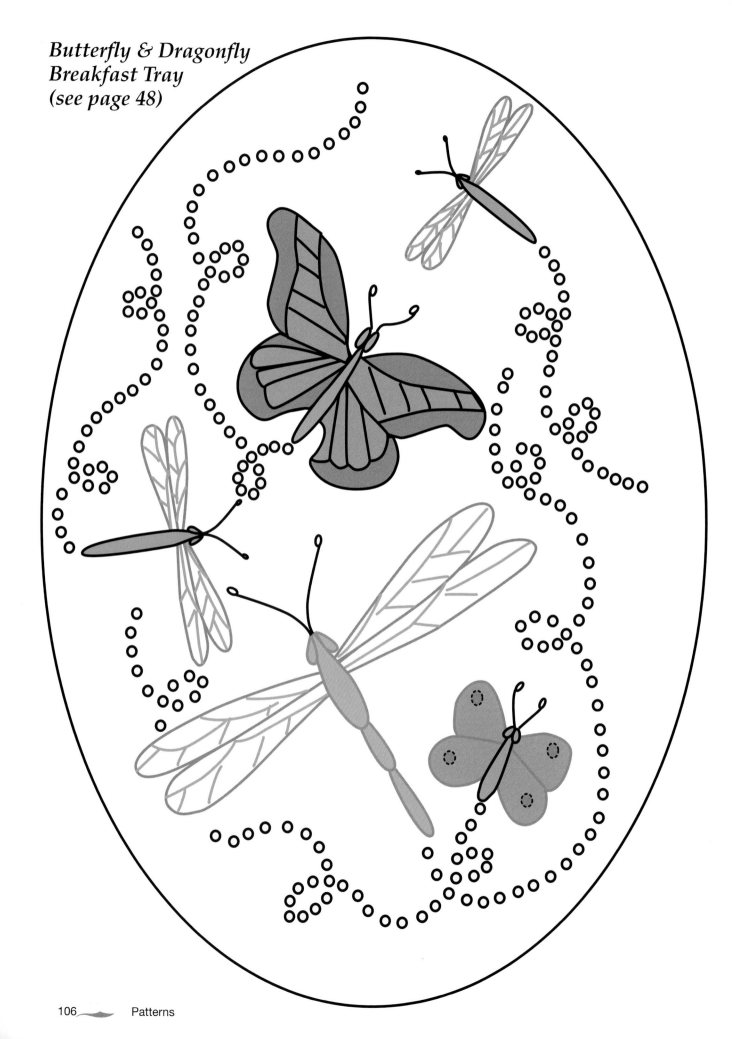

Butterfly & Dragonfly
Breakfast Tray
(see page 48)

God Bless America Sampler (see page 56)

America

A B C D E F G H I J K L
M N O P Q R S T U V W
X Y Z
a b c d e f g h i j k l m n
o p q r s t u v w x y z
0 1 2 3 4 5 6 7 8 9

Eagle Pillow (see page 58)

Eagle Pillow (see page 58)

Rose Heart Pillow (see page 66)

Heart Bell Pull
(see page 68)

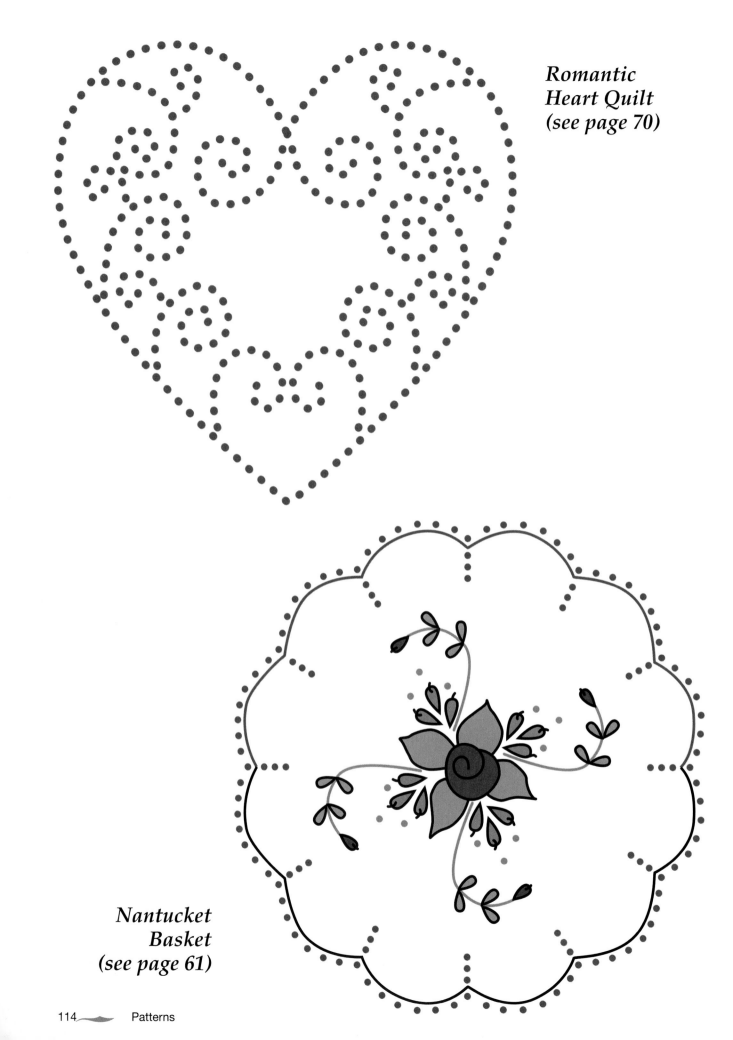

*Romantic
Heart Quilt
(see page 70)*

*Nantucket
Basket
(see page 61)*

Heart Wedding Sampler (see page 74)

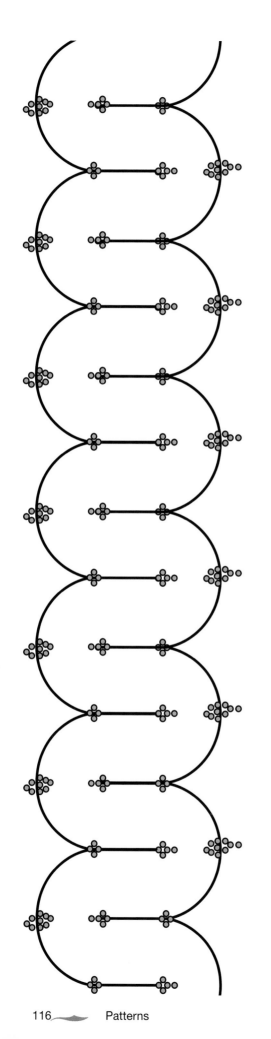

Neck Pillow
(see page 78)

Duck Blanket
(see page 94)

Envelope Pillow
(see page 82)

Square Pillow (see page 80)

Vintage Frame #1 (see page 84)

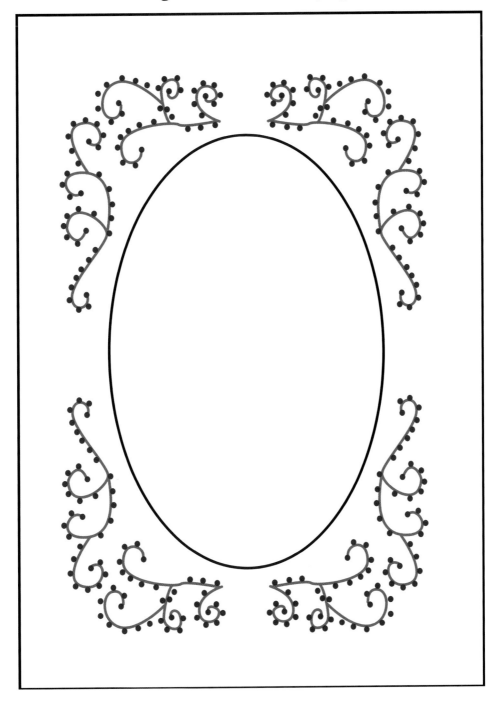

Vintage Frame #3 (see page 84)

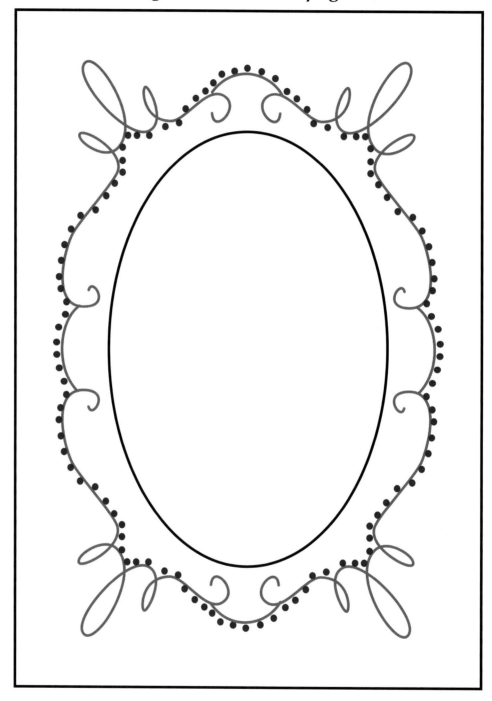

Vintage Frame #2 (see page 84)

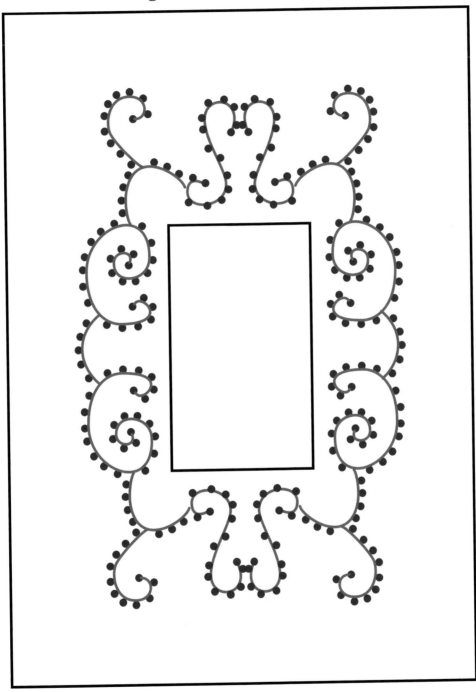

Oval Framed Bouquet
(see page 86)

Baby Girl Sampler (see page 90)

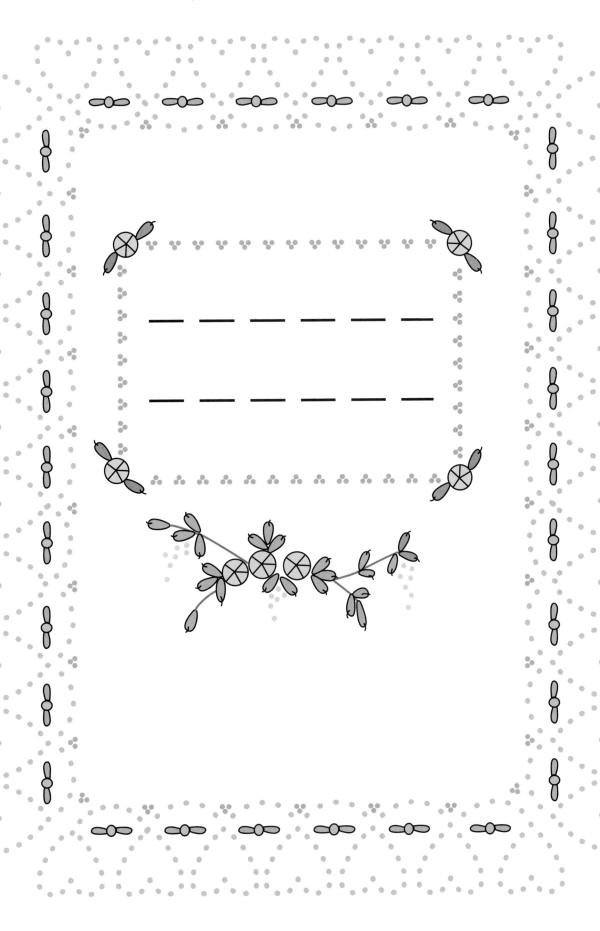

Baby Boy Sampler (see page 92)

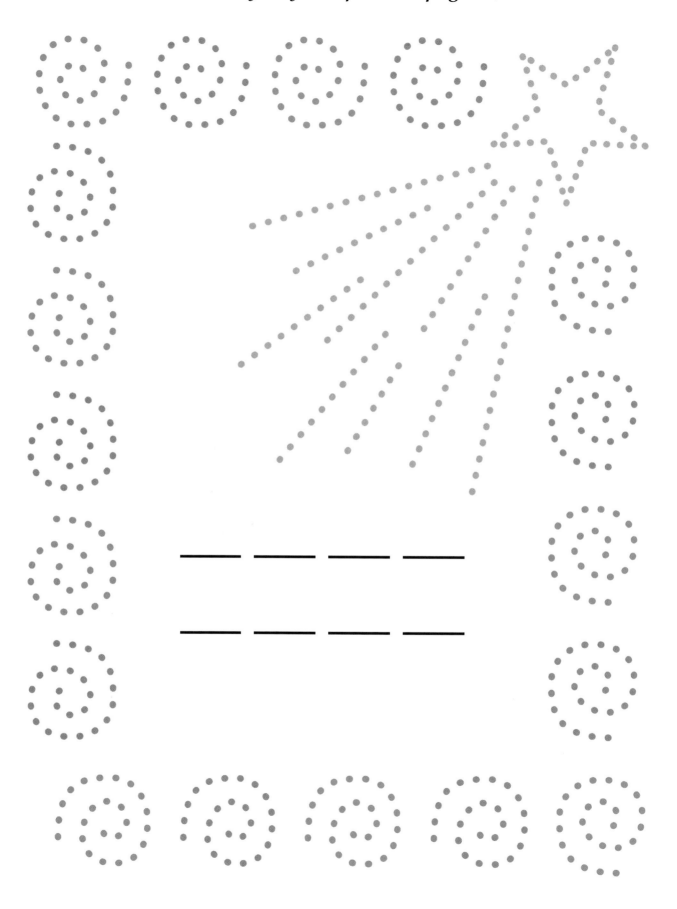

Baby Sleeping Pillow (see page 96)

Resources

Bucilla/Plaid Enterprises
1-800-392-8673
www.plaidonline.com
4mm, 7mm, and 13mm silk ribbon

Charles Craft, Inc.
P.O. Box 1049
Laurinburg, NC 28353
1-800-277-0980
www.charlescrafts.com
dish towels and 100% linen fabrics

DMC Corp.
973-589-0606
www.dmc.com
floss, pearl cotton threads, and even-weave fabric

Fairfield Processing Corp.
1-800-980-8000
www.poly-fil.com
Soft Touch® Poly-fil® pillow forms and batting

Fiskars School, Office & Craft
7811 West Stewart Avenue
Wausau, WI 54401
800-950-0203
www.fiskars.com
quilting and sewing tools

Krause Publications
700 East State Street
Iola, WI 54990-0001
888-457-2873
www.krause.com
books

Sudberry House
12 Colton Road
East Lyme, CT 06333
1-800-243-2607
www.sudberryhouse.com
mirrors, boxes, and trays

Wichelt Imports, Inc.
N162 Hwy. 35
Stoddard, WI 54658
1-800-356-9516
www.wichelt.com
linen fabrics

YLI
1-800-296-8139
www.ylicorp.com
4mm, 7mm, and 13mm silk ribbon

About the Author

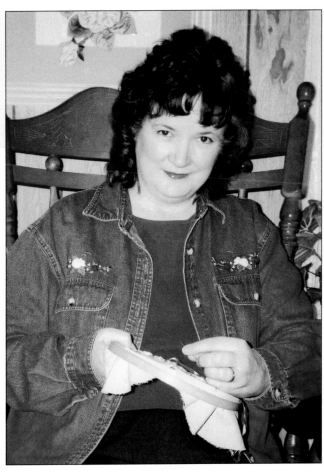

With over eight years experience in the craft industry, Denise Giles is a professional designer, teacher, demonstrator, and ribbon artist. The majority of her designs are in ribbon embroidery and ribbon crafting. Her career began in the mail room of a craft magazine where she was given the opportunity to become an in-house designer, which gave her the start to her designing career.

After a year as an in-house designer, she started free-lance designing and joined the Society of Craft Designers, which opened up new opportunities and allowed her to work with many different publishers and manufacturers.

Denise's projects have been published in many magazines and books, and several have been features on the front cover. Her designs have been published in major craft magazines such as *Arts & Crafts*, *Craft*, and *Country Market Place* magazines. Denise has co-authored two needle tatting books and a ribbon art book. She has worked with many manufacturers in the industry creating project sheets, project samples, display designs, and demonstrations.

Denise enjoys working in many mediums including ribbons, threads, fabric, paper, faux finish painting, leather, and air-dry clay. Her favorite medium is ribbon, and she enjoys experimenting with it in non-traditional ways by combining it with paper, painted surfaces, or other needle arts. The beautiful daffodils, dogwoods, roses, and wildflowers that grow in East Texas provide great inspiration for her designs.

Denise grew up in Dallas and moved to East Texas near Tyler. She has been married to her husband Gary for 28 years, and has one son, Daniel.

HUNDREDS OF PROJECTS FOR
Creative Embroidery

Shay Pendray's Inventive Needlework
Techniques and Inspiration for Gold Work, Painted Canvas, & Shading
by Shay Pendray

Learn the basics of needlepoint stitching, plus couching techniques, combining counted needlepoint stitches with embroidery, and how to use silk and metal on canvas-including types of silks and when and where to use silks. Follow the color photographs and step-by-step illustrations to learn the award-winning stitching tips and techniques of author and needlepoint designer Shay Pendray.

Softcover • 8-1/4 x 10-7/8 • 144 pages
200 color photos & illus
Item# INDL • $21.99

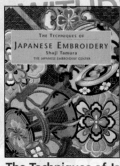

The Techniques of Japanese Embroidery
by Shuji Tamura

Create beautiful traditional Japanese embroideries using detailed illustrations and diagrams for more than 50 stitching techniques. Designs range from flowers, trees, and birds to more abstract works with information on how to create curves, angles, and texture. Metal threads are an integral part of the designs.

Softcover • 8-3/8 x 10-7/8 • 128 pages
150 illus. • 90 color photos
Item# TJE • $23.95

Chinese Embroidery
Traditional Techniques
by Josiane Bertin-Guest

Traces the history of this ancient craft and provides you with the information you need to achieve these beautiful designs-including the necessary tools, techniques, and fabrics used. With clear instructions, step-by-step illustrations, and line drawings, you will learn the most unique elements of Chinese embroidery, including the double-sided and double-faced techniques.

Softcover • 8-1/2 x 11 • 128 pages
150 color photos
Item# CEMB • $24.99

The Embroiderer's Floral
Designs, Stitches & Motifs for Popular Flowers in Embroidery
by Janet Haigh

You'll learn how to embroider 40 different gorgeous flowers in this detailed reference book. From roses and dahlias to geraniums and water lilies, you'll learn through step-by-step instructions how to stitch these popular designs onto clothing or home décor items. Includes an exquisite gallery of ideas to inspire your creativity.

Softcover • 9 x 10 • 160 pages
200 color photos & illus.
Item# EMBFL • $24.95

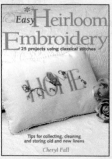

Easy Heirloom Embroidery
by Cheryl Fall

Create items in the style of fine vintage linens using simple elegant stitches. Detailed stitch diagrams will guide you through all the necessary steps to create over 25 projects, many of which can be completed in a few hours. Projects include table runners, dresser scarves, a tote bag, apron, pillows, and framed art. Also included are helpful tips for collecting, cleaning and storing both old and new linens.

Softcover • 8-1/4 x 10-7/8 • 144 pages
200 color photos & illus.
Item# HEMB • $24.95

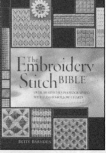

The Embroidery Stitch Bible
by Betty Barnden

Discover 200 stitches designed to add new dimensions to embroidery and improve your technique. Each stitch is photographed and accompanied by easy-to-follow charts and detailed instructions in this spiral-bound guide. Stitches are arranged according to use, including outlines, filling stitches, isolated stitches, motifs, edgings, hems, insertions, flat stitches, backgrounds, and textures. Find specific stitches easily with the stitch selector. Also includes a glossary of embroidery stitches and techniques.

Hardcover W/Concealed Spiral • 5-3/4 x 7-3/4
256 pages • 200 color photos & 400 color illustrations
Item# ESB • $29.99

---

kp krause publications

Offer CRB4

P.O. Box 5009, Iola WI 54945-5009 • www.krausebooks.com

To order call **800-258-0929** Offer CRB4

Please add $4.00 for the first book and $2.25 each additional for shipping & handling to U.S. addresses. Non-U.S. addresses please add $20.95 for the first book and $5.95 each additional. Residents of CA, IA, IL, KS, NJ, PA, SD, TN, WI please appropriate sales tax.